Sweet Nata

Sweet Nata

GROWING UP IN RURAL NEW MEXICO

Gloria Zamora

UNIVERSITY OF NEW MEXICO PRESS | ALBUQUERQUE

© 2009 by the University of New Mexico Press
All rights reserved. Published 2009
Printed in the United States of America

First paperbound printing, 2011
Paperbound ISBN: 978-0-8263-4635-3

17 16 15 14 13 12 11   1 2 3 4 5 6 7

Library of Congress Cataloging-in-Publication Data

Zamora, Gloria, 1951–
Sweet nata : growing up in rural New Mexico / Gloria Zamora.
    p. cm.
ISBN 978-0-8263-4634-6 (hardcover : alk. paper)
1. Zamora, Gloria, 1951—Childhood and youth.
2. Zamora, Gloria, 1951—Family.
3. Hispanic Americans—New Mexico—Biography.
4. Country life—New Mexico—History—20th century.
5. New Mexico—Social life and customs—20th century.
6. New Mexico—Rural conditions.
7. New Mexico—Biography.
8. Corrales (N.M.)—Biography.
9. Cookery—New Mexico.
I. Title.
F805.S75Z36 2009
978.9´57053092—dc22
[B]
                    2008048663

Book design and type composition by Melissa Tandysh
Composed in 10/14 ScalaOT • Display type is ScalaSansOT

To all my grandchildren

Amadeus

Paul

Kiyana

Elijah

Payton

Aaliyah

These words are for you—Te amo, porque sí

Always remembering my husband and truest friend

Until death did we part, my love

Contents

Acknowledgments

First I would like to thank all the characters in my memoir. Each one has enriched my life in many ways. Thank you, Mike, my beloved husband, for all your support and trust in me, your "You can do it, Glor." Says more than you know.

I would like to thank Judy Fitzpatrick for her patient instruction, ever the great teacher; Susan Wyatt for her command of the English language; Regina Zavier for her sincere interest in my stories; Lisa Lenard-Cook, who got it, and for believing in me; Julie Shigekuni, who said such encouraging words and took the time to read my manuscript in its early stages; Rudy Mierra for convincing me to send out my work; and Elizabeth Hadas, whose recommendation helped tremendously. Thank you, Lisa Pacheco, editor, UNM Press; and finally, those who worked with me on the book design, and Diana Bryer for her beautiful art.

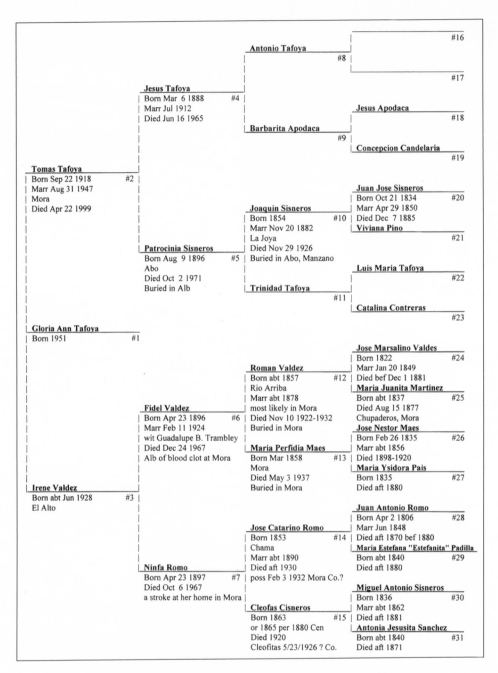

```
                                                              |                           #16
                                          Antonio Tafoya      |
                                                        #8    |
                                                              |                           #17
                    Jesus Tafoya                              |
                    Born Mar 6 1888      #4 |                     Jesus Apodaca
                    Marr Jul 1912            |                                            #18
                    Died Jun 16 1965         |
                                          Barbarita Apodaca   |
                                                        #9    |
                                                              |  Concepcion Candelaria
                                                              |                           #19
  Tomas Tafoya                                                |
  Born Sep 22 1918      #2 |                                     Juan Jose Sisneros
  Marr Aug 31 1947         |                                     Born Oct 21 1834         #20
  Mora                     |              Joaquin Sisneros    |  Marr Apr 29 1850
  Died Apr 22 1999         |              Born 1854      #10  |  Died Dec 7 1885
                           |              Marr Nov 20 1882       Viviana Pino
                           |              La Joya            |                           #21
                    Patrocinia Sisneros   Died Nov 29 1926   |
                    Born Aug 9 1896     #5 | Buried in Abo, Manzano
                    Abo                      |                   Luis Maria Tafoya
                    Died Oct 2 1971          |                                          #22
                    Buried in Alb            |
                                          Trinidad Tafoya     |
                                                        #11   |
                                                              |  Catalina Contreras
                                                              |                           #23
  Gloria Ann Tafoya
  Born 1951           #1
                                                              |  Jose Marsalino Valdes
                                                              |  Born 1822                #24
                                          Roman Valdez        |  Marr Jan 20 1849
                                          Born abt 1857  #12  |  Died bef Dec 1 1881
                                          Rio Arriba          |  Maria Juanita Martinez
                                          Marr abt 1878          Born abt 1837            #25
                    Fidel Valdez              |              most likely in Mora    Died Aug 15 1877
                    Born Apr 23 1896     #6 | Died Nov 10 1922-1932    Chupaderos, Mora
                    Marr Feb 11 1924         |  Buried in Mora     Jose Nestor Maes
                    wit Guadalupe B. Trambley|                   Born Feb 26 1835        #26
                    Died Dec 24 1967         |                   Marr abt 1856
                    Alb of blood clot at Mora  Maria Perfidia Maes   Died 1898-1920
                                          Born Mar 1858   #13  |  Maria Ysidora Pais
                                          Mora               |  Born 1835                #27
                                          Died May 3 1937       Died aft 1880
                                          Buried in Mora
  Irene Valdez                                                |  Juan Antonio Romo
  Born abt Jun 1928   #3 |                                       Born Apr 2 1806         #28
  El Alto                 |               Jose Catarino Romo  |  Marr Jun 1848
                          |               Born 1853      #14  |  Died aft 1870 bef 1880
                          |               Chama                  Maria Estefana "Estefanita" Padilla
                          |               Marr abt 1890          Born abt 1840            #29
                    Ninfa Romo                |             Died aft 1930     Died aft 1880
                    Born Apr 23 1897     #7 | poss Feb 3 1932 Mora Co.?
                    Died Oct 6 1967          |                   Miguel Antonio Sisneros
                    a stroke at her home in Mora                 Born 1836                #30
                                          Cleofas Cisneros    |  Marr abt 1862
                                          Born 1863      #15  |  Died aft 1881
                                          or 1865 per 1880 Cen   Antonia Jesusita Sanchez
                                          Died 1920              Born abt 1840            #31
                                          Cleofitas 5/23/1926 ? Co.   Died aft 1871
```

Tafoya/Valdez family genealogy chart. Courtesy of Katherine Valdez.

Part I

| *1951–1957* |

In the Beginning

I wake to find myself alone in this room with a bed in every corner. One each for me, Aunt Viola, my maternal grandparents, and the one left vacant when grown children moved away. Uncle Eloy, now a high school junior, sleeps in the next room, the one between where I sleep and the kitchen. From his room three wooden steps lead up to a door into what I call the fancy room, where a four-poster bed, a dresser with a bench, and a stuffed sofa and stuffed chair upholstered in the best gray fabric await special visitors. That room remains closed off to my playful adventures but is where Grampa Fidel Valdez naps on the floor or sofa when he has had a busy morning in the fields or on the ranch. He spreads a sheet over the sofa first, of course. Grama Ninfa Romo Valdez reminds me often, "Don't play on that sofa. Your daddy made that, and it is very special to me."

Our bedroom also has a rocking chair where Grama sits to read me story after story and where she looks through her crochet magazines to select her next pattern. A click of her tongue indicates she has found just the pattern, and she proceeds by selecting a ball of thread from a basket full of colorful choices. She then picks out the needle she will use for the next hour or so. After Grama starts her new doily, she may pull it apart, finding it does not look like the one in the magazine. When she is on the right track, she begins to hum. Grama hums hymns all day as she works. It is as habitual as her sniffling and her breaths. Sometimes the hum is accompanied by words and other times it is a soft whistle let out between her teeth, almost like a swirl of s's flowing through the air in familiar tunes.

I wish I could whistle like Grama. I try, but the air I blow returns to my ears, tuneless. I will keep trying until I sound like her.

Grama has two *petaquías*, trunks. One stores extra *cuiltas*, quilts she makes. The other is full of things she loves to look at. "This is my wedding dress," she says as she pulls out a beautiful off-white dress that she puts over her bodice.

Las Aguitas, New Mexico. My grandparents Fidel Valdez and Ninfa Romo Valdez lived in both houses after their marriage in 1924. Photo taken in 1995, courtesy of Gloria Zamora.

"I made this *nagua* out of flour sacks." The slip I see is so pretty that I cannot imagine it was created out of flour sacks, except I have seen how she makes hankies. The slip is crocheted at the bodice and the sleeves and has a long scalloped fringe at the bottom.

Almost reverently, she picks up a veil, which has wax flowers and petals for a crown. A boutonnière made of the same flowers, long white gloves for a woman, another pair that Grampa wore, and white stockings. She says, "I am saving this *tápalo* because it belonged to my mother." The black shawl has long black fringe. Grama puts it on me to show me how heavy it is. Together we look at a maroon hard-covered photo album with pictures of people from long ago.

Every morning I wake to soft light coming from the south window through lace curtains and the smell of coffee and oatmeal and the sound of a crackling fire and the *ranchera* music coming from the large shortwave radio on top of the refrigerator. I can hear Grama talking to Grampa. The quilts I'm snuggled under are heavy and warm. I stretch and quickly reverse my movements away from the cold sheets. I finally jump out of bed when I hear the two of them laughing. I hurry through Uncle Eloy's room into the kitchen. Both Grama and Grampa turn to greet me. "*¡Mira quien viene aquí!*" Like they didn't expect to see me.

"Who else would I be?" I ask.

First one and then the other lift me up high for a kiss. Grampa sometimes rubs his whiskered face on my neck. I laugh or complain, depending on the day of the week—on Sunday mornings his skin is smooth and soft. He asks me the same question every morning, "*¿Quién te ama?*" He has instructed me forever to answer, "*Tú.*" It's true he loves me. Then he asks, "*¿Porqué?*" I answer, "*Porque sí.*" He loves me just because. Then he asks, "*¿Cuánto?*" I stretch my arms out to each side as far as I can to show him how much he loves me. He finally puts me down.

It is hard for me to believe that when I first arrived, I cried all the time. At least that is what I am told. I can't remember. I was only eighteen months old. Menencia teases me every time she sees me. "*Hay viene la llorona de Las Aguitas.*" I don't think she'd like it if I called her the crybaby from El Alto, the place where she lives. My tío Manuel, her father-in-law, always corrects her. He says, "*No eres la llorona de Las Aguitas. Eres la Gloria de todo el mundo.*" I would rather be the glory of the whole world than be called a crybaby.

I do cry sometimes, of course. Grama comforts me whenever I cry, especially when I have earaches. She holds me and sings "Arru Arru Arru" to the tune of "Tura Lura Lural (That's an Irish Lullaby)." She has sung that for as long as I can remember. Her remedy for my earaches is *punche*. She chews the large tobacco leaves and plugs my ear with them. Other times she blows the smoke from the tobacco into my ear through a cone she made out of newspaper. It is odd to see her smoke. She attempts to heal my pain by putting drops of warm tobacco juice into my ear. Vicks and the hot water bottle seem to help a little bit too, but I keep getting earaches. Along with earaches comes the runny nose. Grama sings, "*Cuando yo estaba chiquita me decía mi mamá*, pretty baby, pretty baby, *pero ahora que estoy grande me dice mi mamá, moco verde, moco grande.*" She smiles and wipes away the unwanted mucus with a hanky she carries in the sleeve of her dress. Grampa is the one who changed the words from being a pretty baby to a big green booger. We all laughed the first time I heard him singing it to me.

I also cry when my stomach hurts. She gives me *café con canela*. The cinnamon in coffee with sugar tastes good and does help. She makes me *poliadas* to settle my stomach, toasting flour and mixing it with sugar, cinnamon, and water, making a pastelike concoction that will cure the stomach flu the first time I eat it. I like the way it tastes, and it makes my troubles disappear. Grampa takes flaxseed for his stomach; he should try café con canela.

Grandma Patrocinia, my paternal grandmother, gives me *atole*, a runny blue corn meal soup, when she visits and my stomach hurts. When I have a cold, she rubs *manteca y sal* on my chest. She claims the lard and salt will help the cough and chest pains go away.

For my cuts and scrapes or blisters Grama uses *osha* to keep infection away. The smell makes me think of some place long ago, maybe even before Jesus and church. It clears my breathing and my head. Comforting. Osha is always in the cupboard.

Comfort is my Grama. She is with me when I am afraid or hurting or having fun, and I know she loves me even when I am bad.

I am sitting on the *tarima*, a bench Grampa made, by the south window, shaded by pots of large pink, red, and white geraniums. I am watching my grandparents work over the cast-iron cookstove. Grama reaches for the *nata* in the refrigerator. She separates the floating cream from the milk every day. No one in the world can make better *chaquegüe* or oatmeal than Grama. I love mush made out of blue corn meal served with warmed milk, and I love oatmeal covered in sweet nata.

I am ready to eat. She hands me my tin bowl coated in porcelain. Painted roses now covered with cereal. I sit with my grandparents in a high chair that helps me reach the table. It was used for all of Grama's kids, including my mother. The small tabletop was removed after the hinges wore out the wood. Now I use the high chair scooted under the kitchen table.

Eloy and Viola have gone to school. They catch the bus down the road. They must leave in the dark; I don't know when, but even this early there is no sign of them. Mostly I see them in the evenings and on Saturday and Sundays.

On Saturday nights Viola curls her hair with homemade curlers. She has saved the band of tin that Grama removes from cans of sardines or coffee. Viola has cut strips of tin into three-inch pieces and wraps each piece in paper. I like watching her twist long brown hair around her curlers and then tie the ends. Viola is always looking at herself in the mirror. She is very pretty. I watch her smile at her own reflection, making the deep dimples appear and showing white, even teeth. I hear her complain about her freckles but I don't understand why. I wish I had freckles.

Eloy teases Viola about her curlers with remarks about aliens and outer space visitors. Sometimes Viola laughs, and other times it turns into a fight.

Grama's Tejaván

Grama's *tejaván* is the attic over the house where Uncle Casey, Aunt Stella, and my cousins Veronica, Danny, and baby Tina lived. I don't know why they moved away. I liked playing with Veronica. Grama used to let me walk over to visit after I'd had my breakfast.

One morning Aunt Stella let me have baby cereal. She had Tina in her high chair, the one Uncle Casey made from beautiful pine with carvings on the part that supports the baby's back. The wood is polished.

Aunt Stella was sitting in front of Tina in her own chair, putting a baby spoon into Tina's mouth. I had to watch. I'd never seen a tiny spoon before, and even that little amount of cereal seemed too much for Tina's little mouth because Stella kept catching the overflow in the spoon.

Aunt Stella must have thought I was hungry because she offered me some of Tina's cereal. At first I said no, but I reconsidered. "Can I smell it?" After smelling it I decided to try some. She poured dry cereal into a bowl and added milk out of a can. I had never seen milk in a can. After adding a spoon of sugar, she handed me the bowl. Smooth cereal slid down my throat so easily and tasted so good. I ate the whole serving.

My aunt laughed at me and said, "You can come for more tomorrow if you want."

I didn't even play with Veronica that day. I went to tell Grama about the great cereal. Grama gave me one of her stern looks. "I don't want you going over there and bothering your aunt. That cereal is for the baby, not for you."

Now the house has only a few furnishings: an armoire, a kitchen table and six chairs, and a bed frame, all furniture Uncle Casey made out of pine and cedar, polished and beautiful. Grama told me they will be back for the kitchen table and chairs. The furniture looks lonely. Grama must feel like that too because she starts to cry when we go into the empty house.

Climbing the wooden stairs to the attic, Grama looks back at me. "Hold on to the rail. These steps are rickety and old." I do as I'm told. She keeps looking back. "Watch this step here. It's loose and it moves." She watches as I climb the step she is concerned about. Grama teaches me how to count the steps. We count together: "Ten, eleven, twelve." We reach the attic door. Grama says, "Hold still while I open the door."

She takes her free hand, the one not holding the *bandeja*, large pan, and unwraps a wire that is tied to a wooden knob. The door swings open. At first I see only darkness. Then my eyes adjust and I see slits of light creep in from the roof and door. Letting go of Grama's dress, my breath changes. My head tilts upward and I breathe deeply, turning from side to side, sniffing and concentrating, almost doglike. Grama laughs. She surprises me; I like to hear her laugh. She puts down the bandeja she has been carrying and pulls off a see-through netting cover. "Here," she says, "eat this." It is a dry plum. She tells me that dry plums become prunes. I love prune pie. Grama makes the best pies.

"Can I have more?"

"Get as much as you want."

Grama turns each plum over one by one. "We have to check every single plum to make sure it dries properly and does not rot."

She moves to another section and starts to turn apricots that lie in halves on a table made of boards. She grabs a few handfuls and puts them in her pan. Then we move to a table of wrinkled apple slices cut into circles and add those to her tray.

"Grama, how did all this fruit get up here? Did Uncle Casey leave it for us?"

"When Casimiro moved I decided to use this attic because these stairs are easier to climb than a ladder. Your grampa built them years ago when we lived in this house. We lived in this house when your mama and your tíos were children. When Casimiro came to live in Las Aguitas, we let him use the bigger house for his growing family."

"Why did they move?"

"Your tío got a job working the mines in Ely, Nevada. He needed to work."

"I miss them."

"Me too."

Face scrunched and lips puckered, I mumble, "Mmmm! I like the apples best. They are sweet, but sour too."

I follow Grama to the circles hanging from the ceiling, spinning like pinwheels. On tiptoes and whirling in circles I ask, "What are those?"

"Don't twirl like that. You'll raise dust."

"Sorry."

"They are *calabacitas*." She reaches for my hand. "Come, let me show you something very special." We walk away from the drying squash.

I follow her to a place near the door. I have been so absorbed by the fruit that I do not notice anything else in the attic. A big trunk covered in dust and a big wooden box sit waiting to be opened. Grama picks up an object that sits atop the wooden box. "This is a Victrola." She spins the turntable. "It is like magic that plays music. Better than what you hear on the radio."

She has me at the word magic. Many of the books Grama reads to me are about magic kingdoms, princesses, and magical creatures. I stand idly by, watching her put the Victrola on the floor and open the wooden box. Inside the box are flat black disks. She shuffles through, selects one, places it on the turntable, and cranks the handle. Soft, heavenly music plays, amplified through a hornlike piece.

Grama has my hands in hers and we slowly slide from side to side. She has closed her eyes and we spin ever so carefully to the music. I can't take my eyes off Grama's face. She looks so happy. We stop dancing before the music ends. Grama glides as though moved by a gentle breeze. She is humming with the music. I think she has forgotten I am with her. Gently, she secures the cheesecloth covers over each fruit stack. She picks up her bandeja of fruit and walks to the door. "Ready?"

"The music is still playing."

"We can listen to it climbing down the stairs. It will shut itself off."

Grama has closed the attic door and I can still hear the lovely music, just like she said. We leave the secret room that smells better than the Juicy Fruit gum in Grama's purse. My eyes squint at the bright blue sky. A hawk floats in the blueness like a dancer. Grama is right to call it magic.

Her voice breaks the spell. "You choose what kind of pie we'll make today."

"I'll take prune pie today, apple pie tomorrow, cherry pie the next day, and . . ."

Grama stops me before I can finish. "You mustn't be greedy. Be thankful to the Lord that you are getting pie."

Domingos

I am the only one to get breakfast on Sunday mornings. The others have to fast so that they can go to Communion. Viola walks out the kitchen door, her long dark curls swinging back and forth across her back. Eloy grabs his coat from the pegs by the door and follows her. Grama and Grampa come from the other room, he in his suit and tie, she in her blue and white dress saved for Sundays and a silk bandanna. Grampa puts on his clean Stetson hat and she grabs her purse, then my hand. She never leaves home without her purse, which she clutches on her lap between both hands with drumming fingers.

We all climb into the cab of the Chevy truck. I sit on Uncle Eloy's lap and Grampa drives slowly down the hill over ruts and rocks. Our bodies collide slightly in spite of our best efforts to hold tight. At least the road is not muddy; that is when we slide all over the place. I'm remembering the day I tried to pick a sunflower and nearly got pulled out of the truck the past summer, when suddenly I bounce off Eloy's lap and hit my head on the truck ceiling. I don't know whether to laugh or cry. My grandfather apologizes after a stern scolding from Grama. Eloy makes me laugh when he says, "You flew right up. I think maybe you would have rocketed up to the moon if I hadn't held on to you." I laugh because no one has ever been to the moon.

I rub my head and so does my grandmother, saying, "*Sana sana, colita de rana, si no sanas hoy, sanarás mañana.*" Her rhyme always comforts me when I get hurt because I believe that if I don't heal today, surely by tomorrow I will.

We turn left on the Mora road and go a few miles before turning into the church parking lot. There are cars already parked and more driving around looking for a space. We always park by my tío Facundo's house so we can visit him for a cup of coffee after Mass. Uncle Facundo is my grandfather's brother. He rents a room by St. Gertrude's Church in the winter, and then moves back to his house in Las Aguitas in the summer.

I rush through the front door of the church to get to the holy water before

All aunts and uncles in front of Saint Girtrudes church in Mora, New Mexico, after Mass, circa 1959. Left to right, back row: Sofia Brizal, Mariana Valdez, Ninfa Valdez (my grandmother), Adelaido Valdez, and Tomasita Valdez; middle row: unknown girl on right, Lucille Valdez; front row: Facundo Valdez and Fidel Valdez (my grandfather). Photo courtesy of Manuel Tafoya.

my grandparents. I dip my fingers and splash my forehead, making the sign of the cross. Viola climbs up to the choir loft and Eloy goes to the sacristy. He is one of the altar boys who will serve Mass with Father Rael. I follow my grandparents to the pew where we always sit, very close to the front on the left side by a large pillar that we have to skirt to get to our seats.

The church smells of incense and wax, and musty dust particles dance in the air. Double wooden doors squeak, tempting me to turn and see who enters. A pinch and a look from Grama remind me to face forward, never mind about that silhouette blocking the doorway. The women's heads are covered in flowers, feathers, veils, and bandannas. Everyone bows, kneeling and praying in whispers, holding rattling beads that softly hit the pews.

Grama's fleshy arm is so soft, I close my eyes, push my face into it, and nearly fall asleep. Rita, my cousin, Aunt Viola, and the rest of the choir sing their Gregorian chants, "Dona Nobis Pacem" and "Salve Regina," alto and soprano, in perfect harmony. I am in the presence of living angels.

I watch people kneel at the altar rail to receive Holy Communion. It must be very special because Grama has told me it is the very reason we come to Mass. She said Jesus lives in the communion wafer and helps her be good all week. And I said, "You are always good, Grama."

"No, *hijita*, nobody is always good." Grama calls me her precious child all the time.

"But you never get a spanking or get yelled at like I do."

She laughed when I said that. "Let me tell you a little secret. When I was a little girl, I sure got a lot of spankings."

"Why?"

"For the same kinds of things you get spanked for. Now that I am a grown-up, I go to confession and confess my sins to God."

"Like what?"

She shook her head. "You ask too many questions." I thought she was not going to say anything more. "Like gossip," she said. "I should not talk about my neighbors or anybody in a bad way."

I am thinking about all this when the choir starts to sing a happy recessional hymn. The organ music makes me want to dance. I don't dare. I know what trouble I'll be in if I dance. But I see Grama's body move to the music. She wants to dance too. I can feel it.

The group that assembles outside the church when Mass is over is as significant as the gathering inside. Hugs, kisses, and greetings all over the place. Grampa can't leave without visiting with the whole town. For the smaller kids like me, he puts on a show. He puts his hat over his shoe and kicks it up in the air, then catches his hat with his head. The hat falls right on target. We all clap. I do too, even though I've seen him do it a hundred times.

We walk over to Tío Facundo's house and enter a warm room. A potbelly stove with four chairs around it is in the middle of the room, just waiting for us to sit. The one-room apartment is dark, with only one small window. Tío adds wood and pokes at the fire lighting up the room. His teeth and eyes look bright yellow from where I sit, like the firelight is coming from his mouth and eyes. He pours coffee for the adults and hands me a glass of milk. Viola and Eloy are at choir practice. Grampa and his brother talk about political matters around town and the latest Mora–San Miguel Electric Cooperative meeting. We drive to El Alto when choir practice is over.

It has been Romo tradition to come to El Alto for breakfast after Sunday Mass since Great-grandmother Cleofas and Great-grandfather Catarino Romo were still alive. When they died, Aunt Fidencia, Grama's oldest sister who never married, became the matriarch of the family. She inherited the house and insisted the family gather on Sundays as they had while her parents were living. All the brothers and sisters and their families who live in El Alto, Las Aguitas, Holman, Cordillera, and other communities in the Mora area came to their childhood home for breakfast.

When Aunt Fidencia died, her youngest sister, Mary, stayed living in the house. She became the matriarch of the family. If Grama is strict, her sister Mary is stern, bossy, and gets her way. Grama is the opposite of bossy— she aims to please and loves seeing her only living sister, so we come to breakfast.

We drive to El Alto to Aunt Mary and Uncle Manny's house. Uncle Manny is my father's brother, and Aunt Mary is not only my aunt, but also my mother's aunt because she is Grama's sister. On the way, Grama points at a lady on the side of the road holding her thumb out toward the traffic. Grama whispers so loud that I'm almost afraid the lady can hear her. "There goes that crazy Elena hitchhiking again. She's far from Chinatown, where she lives. I wonder if she's bumming a ride to Texas or California this time."

I look at Grama and I feel heat on my neck and ears. I don't think she was very nice about the lady, Elena. I remember what she told me about gossip and talking about people. I realize for the first time that my grandmother is not always good.

Aunt Mary does not serve the traditional New Mexican breakfast. She usually serves white toast with jelly, hash brown potatoes, bacon, and fried eggs. I like her modern ideas. Her table in the kitchen is big and nine of us sit around it. We pray together before we eat. The noise in the kitchen is loud from so much talk.

Tío Manuel, who lives next door and the one who calls me La Gloria de Las Aguas, walks in with a bottle of homemade *capulín* wine. He claims his wine recipe came from Great-grandmother Cleofas and that it is the best chokecherry wine in all of Mora. He pours a little in glasses for Uncle Manny, also a Manuel, Aunt Mary, and himself. Grama and Grampa do not drink wine or whiskey, and Terry, Rita, Viola, Eloy, and I are too young.

When Aunt Mary and Uncle Manny are out of town, sometimes we go to my green-eyed, beauty-marked Tía Sofia's house in Buena Vista for breakfast. Her *papitas* are crispy, her tortillas thick and soft, the whites of her fried eggs are toasty, and of the red or green chile, I only eat the green. Sofia is so nice and takes time to talk just to me. We go for walks to the river from her house or we sit on the back porch. Visiting her is very relaxing.

I have to say, my favorite Saturday or Sunday breakfasts are my grandmother's. Pancakes with homemade syrup or capulín jelly and cream scraped off yesterday's milk. My mouth gets juicy thinking about sweet nata.

There is no telephone at Grama's house and many a Sunday afternoon she gets visitors. Ernesto, Gina, and three of their seven children arrived about an hour ago. Kenny, May, and I are running all over the mountain, chasing each other and making contact with the adults only when they call for us. Leon is off for a walk up the mountain looking for Eloy.

We see Grama chase a chicken, take it to the woodpile, and chop its head off with an ax. We laugh when the chicken runs around blindly until it falls to the ground. We watch Grama pour hot water from the *calentón* in the stove into a big basin to soak the chicken in.

May holds her nose. "Let's get out of here. Wet feathers stink!"

Ernesto owns a grocery store and they have a butcher shop, so they get all their meat from the store.

May speeds away, but Kenny and I watch Grama pull off feathers, leaving the chicken bare.

The three of us watch Gina cut up the chicken into a billion pieces and fry them. Grama throws three handfuls of flour into a large bowl; mixes in lard, pinches of salt, and baking soda; and adds water. It isn't long before Grama says, "Go get your Grampa and Ernesto to come and eat." Ten of us devour the chicken in gravy and feel perfectly content. The biscuits, fried potatoes, and home-canned peas complete Grama's Sunday meal.

Funerales

Funerals are a time to cry and to remember. Tía Mauricia died. She was Tío Ricardo's wife and Grampa's niece. She had cancer and was in the hospital in Albuquerque when she died. After the *velorio*, her wake, Uncle Manny brought her to the church in his station wagon and then to the *camposanto*. This graveyard is full of Grama and Grampa's relatives.

Grama and Grampa picked all the lilacs off the bushes in our yard and filled the back of the truck. We could smell them all the way to the church. After they put Mauricia into the grave, all my uncles covered the hole with shovel after shovel of dirt until a tall pile of dirt made a mound on top of her. Grama and my tías Maria, Fidencia, Sofia, and Grampa and my tíos Ricardo, Manuel, Miguel, Alfonso, Facundo, Candido, and the other Tío Alfonso all put lilacs over the mound. Mauricia was related to the Romos and to the Valdezes.

Now we are burying Fide, short for Fidencia. We also called her Aunt Mina, short for *madrina*. The name stuck when Julia, her goddaughter, could not say madrina. Every child born in the Romo family after Julia called her Mina.

She was fine last week when we butchered a pig, getting ready to make the Christmas tamales. "One day she's cooking in her kitchen, and the next she dies." That is what Grama said.

We stand out in the cold while they drop her coffin into the hole in the ground. Her grave is next to Tía Mauricia's.

It is horrible to hear all the moaning and loud cries. I can hardly see whose face is behind the tápalos, black capes, and the long black veils. It's spooky.

We miss both aunts very much. Tío Ricardo's house seems very empty without Tía Mauricia. I used to watch Mauricia pull water out of the well and would follow her inside to get a cookie.

Aunt Mary lives in Tía Mina's house, but I miss seeing Mina. She made the best tortillas, dozens at a time—a pile so high it was like a tower of tillas. When the scent of those wonderful tortillas floated into the neighborhood, all her nieces and nephews came for a treat, hot tortillas with butter. In just one seating dozens of her tortillas disappeared.

If she wasn't making tortillas or other food, she was washing clothes in the green wringer machine. The machine made a grinding, twisting sound like it was working very hard to clean the clothes. Hidden from view, her small frame hung white clean sheets on the *percha* to flap in the wind, sounding like clapping hands.

Visitas

We're going visiting today. Chulo, the dog, hurries to us when we come through the kitchen door. The window on the door rattles and shakes, ready to fall out. The window shade on the door scrolls up with a clapping sound that makes me jump. There is no way to sneak out of the house without being heard. I welcome Chulo's licks and wagging tail, but when the red rooster runs toward us, I am watchful. Grama will scare him away with a stick or her purse and Grampa simply kicks at him, but I am defenseless against it. Chased by puffed red feathers, mean staring eyes, and sharp curled claws, I cry, scream, and run from a wicked beak open and ready to pierce.

Grama threatens to kill him and eat him, but it hasn't happened yet. I am even afraid to walk to the outhouse by myself. This monster rooster refuses to let me play in the yard without attacking. Grama makes sure he is in the *gallinero* before she lets me out to play. I never go into the chicken coop to get the eggs for fear of an assault on my life.

Before we begin our visiting, Grampa drives us to the post office, and I already know that we will go for an ice cream cone at Ricardo Branch's fountain. We talk with Ricardo from our table. He is the postmaster too.

Now we are at Tío Miguel and Tía Delfina's house in Cordillera. Miguel is Grama's brother. They have no children living at home, but I like to sit with the grown-ups here in the front room and let my mind make up stories. A knock warns me that someone is at the door. I run for the closet and hide. The voices I hear sound like Aunt Mary and Uncle Manny.

I tell myself it is okay to leave the closet, but I don't. Uncle Manny comes to me and encourages me to come sit with them on the sofa. I shake my head, but he lifts me up and carries me. A man and woman who I don't recognize are sitting on the sofa. Uncle Manny makes me shake hands with them, tell them my name, and then sit on his lap. I feel like everybody is watching me and I don't like it, but I am made to sit there and answer questions. When they leave, I run over to where Grama is sitting clutching her purse, and I grasp her arm but I don't cry, even if I feel like I will.

On the way back from Cordillera we stop at Bercy's house in Mora. She and her husband have a daughter and son who I play with. She serves us coffee, cookies, and peaches. The grown-ups stay inside talking while us kids play in the spring that runs in front of the house.

At Eddie's garage we stop just to say hello. Grampa is not related to Eddie but enjoys talking with him. They know each other from the Unión de San Jose, a church society.

We make what I think is the last stop. Doña Pablita lives in a large two-story adobe house. She is Tío Torivio Maes's daughter. Tío Torivio is Grampa's uncle, but he is already dead. Pablita is always sitting in a rocking chair. There have been times her legs are covered with a blanket. She is very old. I have heard Grama talk about her having seizures. It sounds like she can't control her body and that it can be dangerous because she is alone most of the time.

Grama goes into Pablita's kitchen and makes a fire and then warms beans and chile. She takes food to where Pablita sits in her rocking chair so she can eat. They talk for a while before we leave.

Grampa turns in the direction of home, Las Aguitas, but passes our turnoff. We stop at Tío Candido and Tía Mariana's house. I call him Tío Oso. I think his brothers call him *oso*, bear, because he is tall, muscular, and bearded. They are all tall. Grampa is five foot eight inches and he is the shortest of the brothers except Tío Adelaido, but he is *cojo* from an injury that left his knee bent, and so he walks with a limp and leans to one side.

Tío Oso is my favorite of Grampa's brothers. He teases me and rustles my hair and tickles me. He throws balls to me and he talks to me about the bears and wolves in the mountains. In fact, his dog is part wolf.

Tía Mariana makes Grama uncomfortable. She asks Grama questions that she would rather not answer. It is hard for Grama. She stutters, hesitates, sniffles, and clears her throat, but in the end she is tangled up in gossip.

Tía Mariana is very pretty for an old lady, and her hair is dark black, not gray like Grama's. Mariana tightens her nose and lips as though she smells something bad and then gossips about my other aunts. I don't know what to think of her, but I love Tío Oso.

On our way back to the house Grama complains, "Mariana didn't even offer coffee, much less lunch. I always feed people when they come to visit. There is always enough food. Whether it is beans and potatoes or whatever I have, I offer what I have." It sounds like Grama is not too happy with Tía Mariana.

There are so many people to see on visiting days. In El Alto we visit Lucas and Marcella, Menencia, Manuel and Tío Manuel, Samuel and Lucia, Pancho and Lola, Triviño and his mother, Frutosa.

They tell an ancient story about Frutosa's mother. They say that when Frutosa's mother was very young, a band of Indians captured her and her baby brother. The Indians grabbed the baby boy by his feet and swung him against the trunk of the tree in their yard and killed him. Then they took the girl and rode a few miles up the mountain. After that the young girl would not speak. The Indians tried everything to get her to speak. She bore a scar on her throat where they tried to bring back her voice by cutting her throat. But she never spoke again, not even as an adult.

There are children and cousins to play with at all of these homes except Triviño's and Aunt Mary and Uncle Manny's. It is easy to see everyone because they all live so close together. In fact, we park at one house and walk to the rest.

At one time the houses were connected in a large U-shape and closed in with large wooden doors. Grama says the patio was large and all the doors from every house opened up to it. She says the reason people built houses like this in the old days was to keep children and wives safe from Indian attacks. My tíos still talk about the old days.

"When we hoed the garden," they say, "Mama would tell us, 'Do not let your hoes hit because the Indians will hear them clink and know you are out in the garden. They will come and steal you away.'"

The garden was outside of the protected area. Sometimes when I am in the fields, I look around for Indians, just in case, but I never see any. Still I am afraid and do not go back there alone.

In Mora we visit Tía Tere, Ernesto and Gina, the Ganderts, and Bercy. All their houses have a stream running in front by the road. I like to play in the water and watch leaves float away. Sometimes the backyards are swampy and wet.

In Buena Vista we visit Tía Sofia, Grampa's sister, and her daughter, Osma. She lives a little ways from Sofia. Tía Sofia has the Mora River running right close to her house. I like to hear the water flow over rocks when we sit on the porch. I am allowed to cross the river over large and small slippery rocks if Grampa holds my hand. I don't get to cross over to the other side every time we visit, but we always take a walk along the river. I like the smell of *jarita* from the river brush.

Don Perciliano Lucero and his wife, Tía Sofia's neighbors, have very pretty things in their house, like cupboards full of china and very fancy furniture. I like to look at the pretty plates and pitchers, but I make sure not to touch anything that can break. I'd get a very big spanking if I touched any of those pretty things.

We are on our way to Las Vegas, not the Vegas in Nevada, but the one in New Mexico, thirty miles southeast of Las Aguitas and Mora. We go there to see Grama's doctor, make a stop at the Piggly Wiggly, or go to Penney's Department Store or Sears.

Often we visit doña Otelia, Grama's cousin in some distant way. Otelia lives in a very large two-story house with her husband, Manuel. They have two inside bathrooms. The toilets flush and the tubs have faucets for water to fill them with. The sinks in the house also have faucets where we can get water for drinking or washing our hands.

Our *común* at home is a two-hole outhouse. We have to walk through the yard, then through the plum trees, all the way back to the fence that separates Grampa's property from his brother Tío Adelaido's.

We have plenty of privacy, but it is scary for me to go alone at night. Grama makes me hurry and never points the flashlight in the right direction. She gets upset with me because I'm scared and tells me, "*Tienes que tenerme miedo a mí, yo tengo la faja.*" I do not take her seriously. She can threaten me and say she is the one I should fear because she has a belt, but I know she will not use it. To wash our hands we walk all the way back to the kitchen and use the *aguamanil*, the basin on a washstand.

Before we even knock on Otelia's door, we climb four long steps to a porch. On one side of the porch a two-seater swing hangs from the porch ceiling. The trim around the windows, the pillars, the floorboards, and the double doors are all painted bright white. Etched glass on the doors makes a very nice design. The rest of the house is green.

We enter the front room and to our left are two sofas and a stuffed chair, a rocking chair, lamps on matching tables, and a rug over the hardwood floor.

To the right is the room where Otelia sees her patients. She is a *curandera*, a healer. Sometimes when we drop by the door is closed, but I can still smell herbs brewing in there or burning weeds or incense. She is also the *partera* who delivered all of my grandmother's children, nieces, nephews, and many others. People in Mora depended on her aptitude as a midwife for many years.

We are invited into the kitchen where Otelia makes tea or coffee. To get to the kitchen we walk straight ahead through a dining room with a large table and matching chairs. A very pretty light hangs over the table from the ceiling. We enter the kitchen through a swinging door. We sit at another table, painted yellow with green trim, and talk while the drinks are brewed.

Usually I am with Grama or Grampa, but today I stayed with Otelia and Manuel. I don't know why. I follow Otelia around the house as she dusts her furniture with polish and cleans her toilets with a brush and some Ajax. I don't like the smell of Ajax.

Otelia's patient just arrived for treatment. She and Otelia go into the healing room. Sometime during her stay Manuel shows me a second set of stairs leading to the upstairs from the kitchen. The passage is dark, very narrow, and steep, not wide and straight up like the stairs from the front room. A few steps up, he flips on a light switch. I feel closed in.

Manuel takes my little hand in his and leads me to an attic with two windows. We walk over to one and look out. He points at the train tracks, then at the round house. "That is where trains are repaired." He says that a train will be coming through soon and makes it sound exciting. We wait and sure enough we hear the train whistle and the chuga-chug of a train. I follow his lead and cheer to see the train.

I don't know how it starts, or why, but his hands pull down my panties. I freeze. He touches me and I stare at him but say nothing. He turns me so that my back faces him and I cannot see his face. I can hear his heavy breathing. He holds my head so that I am unable to turn and look at him. He lowers me to the floor and lies beside me, still facing my back. I feel flesh against my legs. I am so quiet and still.

After that, there are several more visits to the attic to look at the trains. In my innocence, I am as excited about it as Manuel is. Sometimes we use the outside stairs. Eventually the day came when my grandfather joined us in our visits to the attic. Manuel never played the game when Grampa accompanied us.

One day when we got home, Grampa's voice became rough and his face turned red and he screamed and chased the red rooster, grabbed him, walked with long hard strides to the woodpile, and chopped his head off. The rooster ran around wildly for a while with no head, almost as angry as Grampa, never to bother me again.

Día a Noche

Morning to night, the days are full. Snow is on the ground, on the tree branches, on the roofs of houses, and on Grampa when he walks in the kitchen door. He holds two rabbits by the hind feet, leaving the heads to swing as he walks straight for the stove to warm up. "Here's dinner."

Grama quickly responds with, "*Sho*, get those rabbits outside. I'll dress them in a little while."

Grampa has been out all day. He started early this morning when he milked the cows in the corral and fed them, and then fed the pigs and gave them water. I know this because some mornings I follow along and help him. I have watched my grandfather walk the entire ranch on foot, with both hands clutched behind his back. "Hold your hands back here like this." He always has to show me. "Your hands support your back so that it won't hurt." He could mount Flika, his horse, and ride all over the ranch, but I think he really enjoys his walks.

One time when I followed him up the mountain to check the water for the cows, he climbed a big boulder. I followed him up and up, sometimes crawling and pulling myself up by holding on to weeds, branches, and rocks. Grampa extended his hand if I needed help. Finally at the very top, we looked all around to see the whole of Las Aguitas. A squirrel climbed the tall blue spruce next to where we stood. In a flash he climbed nearly to the very top, and then sat very still, watching us.

Before I knew it, Grampa jumped off the boulder to a second boulder butted up to the one we had climbed. He stretched out his arms and told me to jump down to him. He was quite a distance from where I stood. I refused to jump. A space of a foot or more separated the two boulders, and to me it looked impossible. The second boulder was about three feet shorter. Grampa looked up at me. "Jump. I'll catch you."

I looked to see where we had come from and knew I could not go back without his help. "I'm afraid. What if you don't catch me?"

He shook his head, becoming impatient, and said, "You have to trust me. I won't let you get hurt. I am your grampa. Come on now, jump." He almost had me convinced. I took a breath and was about to jump but lost my nerve. He finally lost his temper. "I can't jump up to get you or I would." His arms stretched high, and because it looked like he might cry, I did it. I took the leap. He hugged me and sounded so relieved, "You see, I told you I would catch you."

Grama prepares the rabbit pretty much like she does chicken. She talks to me about hunting rabbit while Grampa and I play checkers. "It is only safe to eat wild rabbit on the months that have an 'r' in them. Repeat after me: *septiembre, octubre, noviembre, diciembre, enero, febrero, y marzo*." And she is happy when I don't have to repeat but can say the months *with* her.

Sometimes I beat my grandfather at games, but most times he beats me. He reminds me to king him. Almost every evening when Grama is preparing dinner, he plays games with me. In Chinese checkers he teaches me moves that he guarantees will always help me win. We play Cocinita or Cocina Robada with a deck of cards. At first we matched cards that were on the table, but now I can add two of the cards on the table and pick them up if they equal the sum of the cards in my hand. Grampa teaches me how it is done. We play Wajo, a marble game on a game board that Grampa carved out with his knife. We each have four marbles of the same color so we know which marbles are our own. We have a home for our marbles and can only start to travel around the board if we get out of home with a toss of one or six on the dice. We get all the way around and return to another home base to win.

Rabbit in gravy is so easy to chew and tastes so good. After dinner we drink coffee and eat cream-covered bizcochitos, the best cookies Grama makes. I like the cinnamon sugar that covers them, but mostly I like helping Grama cut them into rectangles and curl the edges; this makes them look like fancy crosses. I am allowed to drink a small amount of coffee with lots of milk.

Grampa reads the *cunques*, the coffee grounds left behind in the cup once we finish drinking our coffee. He gives elaborate readings, like a fortuneteller. "Your reading says that you will be very rich one day." He tips his cup over and looks inside. "Mine says that I will find rubies all over my mountain."

"What does Grama's say?"

"Your grama is very lucky. Her future and her present make her very happy because she is married to the man of her dreams."

"*Sho! Tú.*" Grama laughs and shakes her head.

"Will I? Grampa, will I get married to the man of my dreams, like a prince?"

"We have to wait for another reading. Maybe tomorrow the cunques will tell another story."

Grama and Grampa leave the kitchen and go to the bedroom. She is probably crocheting, and he might be starting a fire in the little stove. I can hear the iron door squeak open.

Viola and I wash the dishes every night. I can only dry because the dishwater and the rinse water are extremely hot. The water basins sit on the stove over the burning fire and even get too hot for Viola's hands. Sometimes she moves the dishpan to the table. I am too little to reach the cupboard to put away the dishes, so after drying them, I place them neatly on the table.

Viola grabs some cups and walks to the cupboard. She and I nearly crash into each other, but we both move aside. I laugh but she doesn't think it's so funny. I watch her walk over to the dishwater, not even a smile on her face. She stands there wringing out the dishrag because we are almost done with our chore. Suddenly she gasps and stares out the kitchen window, eyes wide, and she covers her mouth to hold in a scream.

I look to where she is staring and see nothing but darkness. I don't like the dark, and it is very dark outside. "What is it?" I nearly cry.

"I don't know," she says with fear in her voice, "but I saw something out there."

My legs seem to be in quicksand, and I want to run only to find I am stuck looking at her. Finally I scream and take off to the bedroom.

She catches me and starts to laugh. "There is nothing out there. I'm only kidding." I look at her as if she is a wicked witch. When I cry, she apologizes, and like other times, I forgive her and believe that she will never do this again.

Uncle Casey used to come to the kitchen door and knock when we were doing the nighttime dishes. He'd wait for me to turn toward the door, and then he would light a flashlight, showing his big nostrils and rolled-up red eyelids pressed against the window. I'd cry and he'd laugh. I never got used to his pranks, his word for what he did.

Spooking me is a favorite pastime for the young and old delinquents in

Las Aguitas. Some evenings we walk next door to eat dinner at Tío Adelaido and Tía Tome's house. My grandparents play cards with my tíos. After cards we walk home in the dark. Their kids are old. Two are in high school and the others have graduated or are married. Angela is about to graduate and thinks she is funny when she tells me, as we are leaving, "Watch out for *gavilanes* and *tecolotes*. They steal little girls." Hawks steal our chickens, and I can hardly see the large night owls' strong wings when they fly by. I do not wish to be stolen by either bird and stick close to my grandparents as we walk home.

Grama reads "Cinderella," a story out of the big book with many fairy tales. I dress in my pajamas and we kneel on the rug by my bed. We pray, "*Angel de mi guardia, dulce compañía, vela me de noche y guía me de día.*" Now she is teaching me the prayer in English. "Angel of God, my guardian, dear to whom God's love entrust me here. Ever this night, be at my side to light and guard, to rule and guide. Amen." I repeat this prayer every night. Grama says we all have guardian angels that take care of us all day and all night. She wants me to learn some English, but we never speak it except to say this prayer.

Some nights I am afraid to go to my own bed. Other nights I try to fall asleep but can hear my grandparents playing cards in the kitchen and wish they would come to bed so I won't be alone. I have begged them to let me sleep with them when I am very afraid, and they have allowed it. I sleep between them and hook arms. I hook an arm around his and the other around hers and cover my head with the quilts so I can go to sleep. In the morning I find myself in my own bed and wonder how I got there.

Pila de Maíz

Corn piles reach to the ceiling of this *fuerte*. We have been working on the piles for a week. Grampa has three large one-room log houses that he has built for storage and workshops. Besides corn, there are sacks of pinto beans stored in here. Hay and wheat are stored in another, and all of Grampa's tools are in the third.

Grama and I sit on top of the pile of corn, holding our balance by spreading our legs apart and digging our feet into the pile. We shuck countless ears of corn, throwing the husks into a pile of their own and the corncob to the door where Grampa stands. He throws the corncob into the corn grinder and cranks the large wheel. The metal squeaks, in need of oil. The kernels crunch and sound like popcorn popping out of the metal before falling into a gunnysack, and the cob falls to the ground. The ground is getting covered in cobs. Those empty cobs are fed to the hogs. By lunchtime there is enough sitting room between the pile of corn and the ceiling. A few more sacks of corn are leaning against the wall, ready to be fed to the farm animals.

Our lunch break is when Grama says "Time to eat." After lunch, I help Grama clean pinto beans and she adds wood to the fire. In bed for an afternoon nap, the rhythmic sh, sh, sh, sh of the pressure cooker sings my very own lullaby. Sh, sh, sh, sh, like a mother's wishful command as she pats her crying infant's back. When I wake up, I find Grama on the pile of corn and Grampa grinding away.

Pila de Colchones

Mattresses are pulled off the bed and piled on the floor. Grama takes them apart at the seams to wash the wool inside. She removes the ticking material to wash, and also washes the wool in hot water with lye soap. It smells like the dog when he goes for a swim. She spreads the wool out to dry on sheets, out by the well, where the sun shines all day. We pray, asking God for sunny days so that it will dry quickly. Every day Grama checks for dryness. She decides when the time is right to turn every piece of wool so that the underside will dry too. Once dry, the pieces of wool are fluffy and no longer matted. Grama stuffs the ticking with clean fluffy wool and sews up the mattresses.

She loves the smell of clean mattresses. The process is repeated until all the mattresses in the house are clean. Grama says, "Next summer we don't have to wash the wool. We'll just take mattresses apart and beat the wool to fluff it up. Only half the work."

A day or two after all the mattresses have been put back on the beds, Tía Mariana and Tío Candido come to spend the night. I don't know what the occasion is because they live just a mile away. Grama shows Mariana which bed to sleep in. Mariana puts on her nightgown and sits in front of the dresser mirror, pulling hairpins out from two buns on the sides of her head. Two long braids hang down her back. She takes each braid apart, drawing dark wavy hair forward over each shoulder, and begins brushing while moving her hand gently over it. Her straight posture and slow deliberate movements remind me of the stories Grama reads about queens and princesses. She is old like Grama, but her hair is still black. She turns to where I sit. "You must always brush your hair every night. At least one hundred strokes."

Grama leaves the room. I think I see her roll her eyes. She never brushes her hair at night. And the only time I see it out of a bun is in the morning when she brushes it, and not one hundred times, then puts it right back into a bun.

I watch as Tía Mariana leans over and peeks under the sheets. Normally I would think nothing of it, but earlier I heard Grama tell Grampa, "Mariana is so nosey. She will probably look under the sheets to check how well I washed my mattresses. She might even smell them. She will, I just know she will."

I don't know how Grama knew this would happen, but I know one thing—my grandmother knows Tía Mariana pretty well.

Pilas de Leña

Woodpiles used for cooking and warming the cold house dwindle quickly. Grampa carries an ax and a handsaw and I follow close behind. If I run ahead, I make sure not to lose sight of him.

We walk quite a distance from the house. A hunk is cut out of the mountain. Grampa said that in 1950 the Nelson Company out of Oklahoma mined for mica and copper. When the company's airplanes flew over my grandfather's property, they detected uranium. "Hot spots" is what they called it. Large bulldozers and backhoes made their way through rocky forest and tore through rocks and land. They paid a $500 deposit to begin the mining process and $100 a month after that. But there was not enough of the mineral to continue to mine, and they left after a few months, leaving a big gap in the mountain.

We have reached the crest of the north mountain. Grampa tells me to look out west. He leans, releases his ax and saw, and points. "There to the right is El Alto; straight ahead are Mora, Holman, and Cleveland. The mountains in Tres Ritos are the highest mountains you can see from here, and behind them to the south is Jicarita Peak in the Sangre de Cristo Mountains."

Looking where he points, I try to find Aunt Mary's house. It is hidden by what we call "Blueberry Hill." Every direction I look is special. The whole valley of Las Aguitas, my great-uncles' houses and fields, cows and horses grazing on yellow grass, snow-covered mountains, green forests, and little towns. "Wow, this is like heaven, we are so high up."

He laughs. "We can see forever."

I think about forever.

"This is where I will build your grama her dream house."

I imagine a fairy-tale castle, large with a moat in front and jesters entertaining us while we eat our dinner.

Two horses pull the wagon up the mountain. Grama is with us. Grampa

At the woodpile, circa 1935. Left to right, back row: nephew, Fidel Valdez Jr., Casimiro Valdez, Bernardino Valdez, and Fidel Valdez Sr. Standing next to Fidel is Francisco Martinez Sr. Sitting in front is a woman cousin and another nephew. Unknown photographer.

said we needed more wood. We have a large woodpile at home, but Grampa insists we need more.

Grampa and I walk from the wagon up the mountain to the *ojito*, little spring, on South Mountain. Grampa's pant legs are scrunched above his untied boots. He leans forward with hands clasped behind his back. The dog runs ahead. The underground spring appears and disappears. At the eye of the spring, Grampa fills the cut-out logs with water for the cows.

Back on the wagon, the horses tow us up the mountain. "Whoa," Grampa says, tugging at the reins. "This is a good place to stop."

Grampa cuts wood. Grama and I help carry it to the wagon. Grama just finishes saying, "Wagon's almost full. I'm grateful for the clouds. It would be too hot otherwise," when a cloudburst makes us run for shelter under the wagon. Large hail hits the wagon hard. The dog joins us. The poor horses just stand there because there is no place to keep them out of the storm. Lightning lights up the now dark sky and I am scared. Grama holds me close. She says, "I sure didn't expect this kind of storm."

The hail stops and only rain continues to fall. Grampa is using rocks to make dams in the arroyo to hold water for the cows.

The storm has passed. Grampa continues to cut wood and Grama helps, but I sit in the wagon, wrapped in jackets, ready to fall asleep. When the wagon is full, the horses take us home.

At home Grama regrets she did not set out pots to catch rain that leaked into the house. She is mopping up the mess. Usually Grampa directs the water outside away from the house and driveway, but today the storm created several small arroyos that ended up making a small lake in the yard. Grampa is not happy about it.

Salidas de Noche

We usually spend nights at home during winter months, except for when we go to Uncle Eloy's basketball games. He is the star of the Mora Rangers. His picture in the newspaper shows him jumping and making a basket. We go to every possible game and cheer loudly. Often I sit with all the teenage cousins and they buy me popcorn and soda. They are the loudest in the gym. There is so much excitement over the games that all of Mora shows up.

Once a month Grampa attends his credit union meeting. He serves on the board, and while he and others attend to business, we visit with women in another room. Some meetings drag on so long I get very sleepy before we go home. Sometimes he goes alone.

Grampa goes to Unión de San Jose meetings, where men pray and find ways to help people in need. Grama and I stay home, unless it is fiesta time, which is celebrated every March. Fiestas mean lots of good food cooked by the wives and shared with everyone in the parish who comes to celebrate the feast day of Saint Joseph.

When we go to wedding dances, Grama and Grampa glide across the dance floor, never missing a beat or bumping into any other dancers. Watching them is like watching a swan swim across the lake with easy, elegant movements, neck extended. They move gracefully as they choose their path around the dance floor. Grama gets tired and sits while Grampa continues to dance with other ladies, mostly relatives, and always returns for his favorite dancer, his wife. I have fallen asleep curled up in a chair waiting for them both to tire and go home.

On summer nights we go to movies in Spanish at the theater in Mora, mostly Westerns. The theater is always full, so Grampa does not like to arrive late.

Bingo nights also attract large crowds. Father Rael comes to bingo wearing his black robes and stops to talk to my grandparents. He laughs a lot.

I like bingo nights for the fun prizes such as lamps and doilies, and for the black-out, they even win money. People talk and laugh and yell "Bingo!" It is always a surprise to see who wins. I am always hoping it will be one of my grandparents.

One bingo was to raise money for the REA to put electricity in the houses that still didn't have it. Grama's house has had electricity since 1949, so we have light every night and only use the kerosene lamps when there is a storm that takes our electric power away.

Life Is So Easy

I am so afraid of electrical storms. Violent pouring rain and hail the size of small eggs bounce off the tin roof, and rainwater gushes in newly formed arroyos that run next to the house. Days turn dark as night. Grama chants prayers and tries to cut the storm with a knife, tossing salt from her other hand toward the sky in a form of a cross. She chants, "*Santa Bárbara, doncella, libranos de rayos y centellas. Santa Bárbara, doncella, libranos de rayos y centellas.*" Her desperate eyes look up into the sky. I wonder if she is afraid, like me. I hope her repeated prayer ritual to Saint Barbara will save us from flashes of lightning and the storm.

Because we have electricity, we now have a refrigerator, which is a good thing because we have lots of milk, cream, and cheese that need refrigeration. I help Grama make butter from the nata. She puts it in a tin measuring cup with a lid and shakes it for a long time. When she gets tired, I help her shake the container. We shake and shake until the nata turns to butter. Grama saves the buttermilk for pancakes and biscuits.

Grama also makes *requesón*, cheese curd, and *cuajada*, yogurt. She adds little rennet pills, or *cuajo*, to a gallon of milk. Cuajo is part of the cow's stomach that she dries to use for this purpose. Cuajo contains enzymes that help milk jell or coagulate and curd. As the milk starts to curdle, she pours it into a flour sack and places it back inside the bowl for a day. The next day, when curdled and formed into a mass, she squeezes out the whey, making a cheese that resembles ricotta or cottage cheese, only more solid. This *queso* can be sliced and eaten with or without sugar, or the way Grampa eats it, with Karo syrup.

Grama makes cuajada in much the same way, except she catches it earlier, before it forms a hard mass, and hangs it from a tree branch to let the extra whey drain. Cuajada is like yogurt. She wastes nothing and saves the *suero*, the whey, as a starter in the next batch of sourdough bread.

We eat cream mixed with anything sweet, like with syrup over pancakes, with capulín or plum jelly over stale bread, and we cover our bizcochitos with it. Grama makes all kinds of elaborate desserts, like Danish with queso. When we have too many eggs and too much cream, we eat cream puffs. We eat simple desserts too, like broken pieces of old bread in our glasses of milk with a little sugar, or *sopa*, made with old bread, caramel, raisins, and cheese. Our cakes and pies are often topped with cream. On bread day Grama makes cinnamon rolls with *pasas*, raisins. She puts raisins in her sweet rice too. She also uses extra milk to make *natillas*, a pudding, sometimes adding bananas and vanilla wafers.

Grama tells me that before refrigerators they put the milk containers down into the well and into the water to keep cold. She says, "We buried cabbage, onions, carrots, and other vegetables underground to keep fresh. Gunnysacks, straw, and vegetables were layered in a hole, and then we covered the hole with dirt."

"Did you eat them full of dirt?"

"We had to wash off the dirt." She shakes her head at me. I know it is because I ask too many questions. "We would dig up cabbage, onions, and even potatoes and whatever else we needed to make a stew. Now, we just open the refrigerator. Life is so easy these days."

She is always saying that.

El Padre

Father Rael is not my teenage relatives' favorite person. He considers holding hands and kissing sins. He preaches to parents, "Make sure your kids do not have boyfriends and girlfriends." Teens are always in trouble with their parents because the adults believe Father Rael. My aunts, uncles, and grandparents try to keep Father Rael from insulting their ability to parent as much as the adolescents work at keeping in good grace with their parents.

I do not go to confession yet, but I overheard my cousin tell another cousin that the priest made her confess that she was holding hands with a boy. She was so mad. "I hate him," she said. "The priest is not supposed to know whose sins he is listening to. And for sure, that hateful man is not supposed to be telling us what our sins are. I can't stand him."

I agree with my cousins that the priest is wrong. But I don't think my aunts or my grandmother would ever believe that a priest is doing any wrong. I wonder who he confesses to? I wonder how he knew it was my cousin in that dark confessional?

Aunt Viola gets in trouble for having a boyfriend. His name is Andy. Grama tells Viola, "I hear from everyone about you and that boyfriend of yours. Don't think you can get away with sneaking around all over town with that boy. I have people watching out for you. It's because they all care about you." Aunt Mary is definitely one of Grama's spies. I think Grama is more upset about what Aunt Mary thinks than what Farther Rael thinks. But either way, Grama gets angry about the boyfriend problem.

Grampa stops the truck on the west side of the church. The nuns live in the convent behind Saint Gertrude's Church. We walk through a metal gate that is painted white. A white rock wall like the one around the church courtyard surrounds the convent too. Convent walls stretch before us and way back on two sides; I can't see where they end. There are many doors and windows.

I follow Grama's determined pace to cement steps leading to an arch carved into the thick adobe and then to a wide door. Her sniffles are coming faster and growing louder. Grampa is waiting for us in the truck.

Once inside, I sit quietly on a large wooden chair looking at my socks. Grama talks to a nun in English. I don't understand what they are saying, but I keep hearing Viola's name. I am looking at all the crosses on the walls and at shiny wood floors. An arched door leads to a smaller room where I can see three more doors. I know the kitchen is behind one of the doors because I can smell food cooking.

Grama and Viola are in the room next to the kitchen. I'm staying out of there. Grama's voice is loud and rough. "You better confess your sins to the priest. You disobey me when you see that boy behind my back."

I hear Aunt Viola say, "Will you give me permission to see him?"

Grama just slapped her. "Don't get a smart mouth on you."

Aunt Viola says something I can't hear, and Grama starts hitting her. She hits and hits. Viola cries and screams, but Grama keeps hitting her. Now they are on the floor and Grama must be straddling my aunt. I think her hands are around Viola's neck. She is choking her. Grampa must have heard Viola's cries or Grama's shouts. Before I am even sure the sound I hear is the door, Grampa is pulling Grama off Viola and yelling, "That's enough!"

I wipe my tears and stand in the doorway, so thankful that Grampa is here.

These are the kinds of things I hear my grandparents talking about late at night: "Mora is full of people that don't mind their own business. If I don't put a stop to Viola seeing the boyfriend, they will say I'm not a good mother."

I hear my cousins say, "Mora is full of spies that butt their noses into everybody's business."

It seems like everybody is trying to be good, but isn't sure what is good enough.

Chíquete

Chewing gum, wherever I find it, goes straight to my mouth. Sometimes, if I beg long enough, Grama hands me the gum straight from her mouth to mine.

Grama carries Juicy Fruit gum in her purse. The smell from her *maleta* is irresistible. When I hear the click of the coin purse or the leather pressed between her hands, I hurry to her side. I rarely get a full piece of gum or even a fresh piece. That doesn't matter. I can smell the already chewed gum, even when it is rolled into a perfect little ball and saved to chew later. I find it on the edge of the shelf in the *trastero*, the cupboard where she keeps pies, cookies, and spices, and I claim it as mine. Good as fresh. When Grama finds it missing, I am the one she hunts for.

"Gloria Ann." The way she runs my names together says everything. She is upset or happy. A singsong "Gloriaaon" is a happy Grama, but "Glorriaaaonna," rolling the r's roughly and an "ah" at the end with a harder accent on the "na" is quite the opposite. Either way I better answer her. There is no pretending I do not hear. I don't think it has much to do with the gum but more to do with obedience. I am not to climb or reach into the trastero, because another time I had climbed up to get the pasas and fell. I cracked my skull and bled. But I love raisins and continue to risk falling and getting into trouble even after that great fall.

Sometimes I try to make a ball out of my chewed gum and save it on the metal bed frame so I will have gum to chew another time. Then I forget about it. When I finally think about chewing it again the gum is hard as a rock and I end up having to throw it away.

Saving chewed gum in my hand for later is a big mistake. I have learned that lesson more than once. Walking into church with gum is grounds for a good pinch, so I save my gum for later. No matter what I try, like holding it with my thumb and forefinger in a little ball, or putting it safely in the palm of my hand, saved gum turns into disaster. Before Mass is over, the gum is sticky, clinging to every finger and making a spider web pattern in my hand. Trying to remove it is impossible. Using Grama's hanky only makes it worse. And after rubbing one hand with the other, I am ready to cry.

Like everyone else who loves chewing gum, I have suffered getting it in my hair. There are remedies for such a tragedy: ice, cold water, alcohol, or scissors. Grama will cut a chunk of hair off if necessary. I have to hear her lecture over and over: "How many times do I have to tell you not to sleep with gum in your mouth. I should just cut all your hair off. Maybe that way you will learn."

Sap or *trementina* from the piñon trees forms hard, but not rock hard, clear balls. Grampa chips them off a branch for me to chew. It takes only a short while before it feels exactly like regular chewing gum with a pine flavor.

A plant with no leaves and thick smooth stems that resembles a tumble-weed without *espinas* grows in the *llanos* in Las Aguitas and Cañoncito. They call the plant *embarañada*. I think maybe it is God's manna in the plains of the desert. Little yellow-white balls form on the branches. The balls are soft inside, having almost a mucus consistency with a slightly harder exterior. We pick several little gummy balls to make a mouthful of chewing gum.

Another plant that grows in the plains looks like parsley and tastes like mint-flavored toothpaste. We chew on that. Uncle Eloy says it is good for clean-smelling breath and when added to the embarañada, tastes and feels like peppermint gum.

Adults like gum, teenagers like gum, and I like chewing gum. Someday I will buy my own packet of gum, just for me.

Fonazo

Fun! Playing is fun. Rocks, dirt, dolls, cards, my duck, canning jars, jar lids, the mountain, and anything that is around me can turn to fun. Water and dirt make good cakes, cocoa, café con leche. *Garambullos, grajellas,* and *moras* are my beans, peas, and whatever I pretend them to be. Gooseberries, currants, and mulberries are the pretend foods I can actually eat.

Grama lets me use my play tin dishes to serve real food that she cooks for lunch or supper. Grampa drinks real café con leche in my little cups. He says I am a good cook, and of course I know it already.

One day I swallowed a caramel by accident. Well, it really was not a caramel; it was a rock that looked exactly like the candy. I was so proud to have found such a perfect rock. I put it in my mouth to suck, and I even said out loud, "This is so good." Before I knew it, it slipped down my throat.

I immediately ran to Grama. "What am I going to do?" I cried. It took a while before I believed her that I would be alright. Grama suggested we look for the rock when I used the bathroom, that it would come out. I wanted proof. For several days I used the *vacín* instead of the outhouse. Usually we used the chamber pot at night when we needed to urinate. After the rock finally appeared, I agreed to use the toilet outside.

That was not the last time I swallowed a rock. I was playing church and the round flat rock looked like a communion wafer. I played the priest giving me communion and somehow it slithered down my throat. I kept quiet about it because I wasn't sure I should be getting communion until after I made my First Holy Communion, when I was older.

I have fun helping Grampa. I follow him to the fuerte and we fix things. One day he showed me how to repair a shoe. It had no holes in the sole after I helped him fix it. Grama tells him to put me to work or I'll make messes. I don't know why she thinks that about me. Sometimes she thinks I can't remember what she wants me to do. Every time I come in or go out, Grama says the same thing: "*Cierra la puerta, cola larga.*" I always close the door behind me—she doesn't have to tell me over and over again.

Walking from Las Aguitas to Cañoncito is one of my favorite things to do with Grama and Grampa. We pick flowers, piñon, and rocks and find clay. We have seen bears twice, and birds, and coyotes. We sing, run, skip, walk slow, then fast, and we stop to let Grama rest. When we get to Uncle Manny's ranch, we have a picnic.

He and Aunt Mary are fixing the old Martinez hacienda that they bought from one of Grampa's faraway relatives. It has many rooms and each room has a fireplace and there are storage bins with small gates. I go in and out of every room and storage bin. I sit by the fireplaces and pretend to warm my hands. In the winter when we walk to their ranch, they light a fire in the stove and we cook and eat inside.

When the weather is warm we swim in the Mora River, crossing over slippery rocks to the swim hole.

One day on our walk back to Las Aguitas, I ran ahead of my grandparents. I was running so fast I tripped and started to roll down into this large ravine. Grampa ran as hard as he could to stop my fall into the big boulders. I held on to Grampa's hand all the rest of the way home and never did that again.

Grampa y Sus Historias

G rampa tells stories about his youth and the time before he married Grama. Eloy asks questions that get my grandfather lost back in the past for hours at a time. It is hard to believe that Grampa was a kid like me or that he lived a life without Grama.

Grampa has a horse named Flika. Flika is gentle and lets Grama and me ride her when we go to El Alto. She even lets Grampa join us on the ride. Sometimes Grampa walks alongside us until we get to the El Alto Bridge. There we get off Flika and he rides to town to pick up the mail while we walk to Aunt Mary's.

Flika has not always been Grampa's favorite horse. His favorite horses were Tejas and John. He told us this story: "Tejas saved my life. A long time ago, I lived all alone in Carrizo, three miles east of Wagon Mound where my father, your great-grandpa Roman Valdez, homesteaded. I took care of the cattle and a few sheep. The house was more like a shack but it kept the rain and snow out and so it was my home.

"It would get very lonely at times. One day, to entertain myself I mounted Tejas and tried to rope a coyote. We nearly had the coyote cornered when my horse fell. I passed out. Next thing I know, I woke up in a strange bed."

I love Flika and our other horses, so hearing about Tejas and John is fascinating, but the other thing he said about waking up in a strange bed scares me. "What happened, Grampa?" I ask.

"I asked the same question, *jita*. Let me tell you. Shortly after I woke up, one of my cousins came into the room. He said to me, 'Boy, am I glad you finally woke up. You have been out for days.'

"I said, 'You're playing with me.' I really thought he was teasing. But he shook his head, left the room, and came back with his mother. 'Tell him, Mamá. Tell him how long he has been here.'

"That's when I asked, 'What happened to me?' I really could not remember.

Roman Valdez and Porfiria Maes Valdez and family, circa 1917. Left to right, sitting: Roman, Pablita (granddaughter), Porfiria, and Arcorciño holding Lucas (grandson); standing: Alfonso, Adelaido, Anives, Fidel, Sofia, Facundo, and Elena (Facundo's wife). Photo courtesy of Ninfa Valdez by a family photographer.

Cleofas Cisneros Romo, my great-grandmother, and some of her children, circa 1901. Left to right, back row: Ninfa, Ricardo, and Alfonso; front row: Maria, Cleofas, and Carlos. Photo courtesy of Ninfa Valdez from Romo family collection.

Catarino Romo, my great-grandfather, who was married to Cleofas Cisneros, 1890. Photo courtesy of Ninfa Valdez from Romo family collection.

"My cousin said, 'We went to visit you and didn't find you home. No big deal because many times we go visit you, you are out checking on the cows or something. But your horse kept snorting and acting crazy.' That horse was my Tejas. Smart Tejas saved my life."

"How did a horse do that, Grampa?" I asked.

"Well, let me tell you, jita. I'll tell you what my cousin told me. My *primo* said, 'Finally we decided that he was trying to lead us somewhere. We followed and found you on the ground, out like a bear in hibernation. Never would we have gone looking for you if your horse had not insisted.'

"You see, that is why I say Tejas saved my life. I am very grateful for my cousins, the Archuletas. They nursed me for a week before I was back to myself again. I will never forget them."

Not all of Grampa's stories are about horses. It is like he was a whole other person before he met my Grama.

We often continued to sit around the table after finishing our dinner to listen to Grampa's stories.

Eloy said, "Tell us about the Pony Express race."

Grampa laughed. "It was like I told you before. The guy who usually won the race every year was showing off. And his rope got tangled up on another rider's horse, so I passed him and won the race."

Then Grampa changed the subject. "By the time I moved back to Las Aguitas, Acorciño and Olivero moved to Carrizo."

"Who are Acorciño and Olivero?" I asked.

Grampa smiled with pride. "They are my older brothers. They took over the ranch when I left to the army in 1918. Then I came to Las Aguitas to help my father here at home. I worked with Papá, ranching and farming. Everyone else except for Sofia was married and Papá deeded his land to Mamá Porfiria. She deeded sections of land to each of her children so they could make a living from it. From spring through winter Papá Roman and I worked from sunup to sundown. The seasons were marked by the work we did, digging, plowing, hoeing, harvesting, saving seed, and plowing again. There was so much land to work, so many cows and horses to feed, so much work."

"What was Papá Roman like?" Eloy asked Grampa.

Grampa was quiet for a little while. He looked into his coffee cup, went to the stove, and served some more. "I can say that he worked hard. He liked

Ninfa Romo and Fidel Valdez, wedding photo, February 1924. Unknown photographer, probably taken in Las Vegas, New Mexico, or by a visiting photographer. These types of photographs were made into postcards.

Fidel Valdez, four siblings, and their spouses, circa 1959. Left to right: Tomasita (Adelaido's wife), Adelaido, Sofia, Candido, Mariana (Candido's wife), Facundo (in back), Fidel, and Ninfa. Photo courtesy of Ninfa Valdez.

his vino and his whiskey. Sometimes he was mean. He often did not come home from town. People used to say he had other women all over town. Mamá hated to hear about that. She would argue with him about it, and it never did any good. *¿Qué va hacer uno?* No?"

I guess Grampa is right to say, what's a person to do, but it is too bad Roman did those things.

Grampa looked sad talking about his father, so I asked, "What else did you do?"

Grampa was happy to change the subject. "Whenever possible, I went to dances. Alfonso played the fiddle and I played guitar. Those nights we were the band. Other times I danced with every lady who would dance with me.

"One time my buddies and I went to watch Balland fight. He would fight local boys. They dared me to go into the ring to spar with Balland, so I did. And before long I was beating him. He was supposed to be good, but I had him beat. That's when they stopped the fight, because they didn't want people to think I was better than him."

Uncle Eloy said, "That's one of my favorites. You all skinny, fighting a guy like Balland."

"I know, son. It is hard to believe even for me."

Looking at Uncle Eloy, Grampa said, "Then, one day I met your mama."

Eloy nodded. "Tell us how you met Mom."

"Well, son, first let me explain a few things. I was away so many years between the army and the ranch in Carrizo that when I met Ninfa we were both old. Ninfa's brother, Manuel, was married to my sister, Anives. Ricardo, your mama's younger brother, married my niece, Mauricia. So Manuel and Anives put us together. I was playing at a dance and I let one of the Pacheco brothers take my place. I danced the rest of the night with your mama. After that dance came many more, and my visits to Grama Cleofas became a pattern until finally we married."

"Who is Grama Cleofas?" I asked.

"She was Grama Ninfa's mother. That makes her your *bisabuela*, or great-grandmother," Grampa answered.

Wow! My grandmother had a mother. Figuring out which of my aunts or uncles is a brother or sister to Grama or to Grampa is not easy. They are all my tíos and tías and I have lots of cousins.

Eloy finished eating and rose from the table to get bizcochitos and nata. We all ate cream over our cookies and waited for more information about the days before Grampa married Grama, but there was no more that night.

Eloy knew how to draw stories out of Grampa, and the following day at dinnertime he asked a funny question. "So, *te dieron las calabazas*, Daddy?"

Traditionally, if the family of the bride did not give permission to marry or rejected the future groom, they would show their disapproval by throwing pumpkins at the man. It is said that some families with slightly more class cook squash for dinner and invite the family to eat, indicating a "no" answer. In later generations it became a joke, as in the way Eloy asked it.

Grampa laughed. "No, I didn't get rejected, but the day of the *prendorio* there was an incident.

"Everyone was so busy preparing for Ninfa's official engagement dinner and paid little attention to Julia. Julia was about five at the time. I can't blame the little girl. Being the first grandchild she was used to a lot of attention,

Grama Ninfa's Romo siblings, circa 1978. Left to right: Alfonso, Carlos (sitting), Ricardo, and Maria. Photo courtesy of Gloria Zamora.

to the point of being spoiled, I think. When my parents and I arrived, of course everyone was busy, and all the attention was on us. I felt like I was under observation.

"Eloy, your tía Luicita sent Cleo for her sister, but no one had seen Julia in quite a while. Ninfa was so nervous that day. She didn't know what to do. I remember she told Cleo, 'Be sure and tell your mother that Julia is nowhere to be seen. I'm sorry, but I have guests and can't help look for her.'

"About ten minutes later, Luicita shows up at the door, saying, 'I have looked everywhere and can't find Julia. Where could she have gone?'

"This time, Ninfa explained to us that she had to go help find her niece. Cleofas and Catarino said, 'Go. Help your sister find that girl. We'll sit here with Roman and Porfiria.'"

Grampa touched my chair, letting me know that he was going to say something to me. "They are my parents, your *bisabuelos*. Anyway, everyone else searched for Julia—Ricardo, Alfonso, Manuel, and even I helped look for her."

"So where did you find her?" I asked.

Grampa put his finger to his mouth. I straightened out in my chair and decided to listen quietly. It was one of those times, I realized, when an adult wanted to be heard with no interruptions.

Grampa repeated, "We all searched for Julia. She told me later that all she wanted was to eat *chicos*, the sweet corn we dried for winter. She said to me, 'I knew the chicos were hanging in the attic. Everyone was busy so I climbed the ladder to the attic all by myself.' She was pretty proud of herself. Then she said, 'It has some missing steps, but I pulled myself up on the nails, the ones that used to hold the missing steps.'

Grampa said, "Can you imagine a little girl, your age, Gloria, climbing up there? She could have gotten hurt. Especially with missing rungs! Promise me, mi hijita, you won't ever climb the ladder."

I blinked my eyes because it never crossed my mind to climb the ladder. Then I raised my brows and smiled. "Never, Grampa. I will never climb the ladder." I started to wonder if there were chicos in our attic.

"Good," he said, and continued his story. "Anyway Julia said to me, 'When I heard everyone calling for me, I almost said, "I'm right here." But then I knew I was in deep trouble for being in the attic. Then it was kind of funny that nobody could find me.'

"I remember," said Grampa with a smile on his face, "Alfonso noticed the attic door was open and didn't think she would be there but decided to check just in case. He didn't find her.

"Julia admitted she heard someone come through the attic door and hid behind the bins of wheat. 'I even held my breath,' she said. *Que muchita.* That was one spoiled little girl."

Grampa shook his head and looked at Grama. Grama added, "Yes, she was, but she was so cute. We could not help it."

"So we looked everywhere," Grampa began, "even in the well, just in case she had fallen in. I walked down the road calling for her. I went to the *ojo caliente*, but there was no sign of her at the hot springs. Manuel knew Alfonso had checked the attic but decided he would take another look. As he walked around the bins, Julia crawled, hiding from him. Manuel saw a flash of Julia's red dress, picked up his pace, and grabbed her. This time we had her.

"You know, we can laugh about it now." Grampa tapped Grama on the hand.

Grama nodded, then shook her head. "But that day we were not laughing. We were all so mad at that poor girl."

Grampa looked at me. "I tell her all the time that because of her, I almost didn't get married. She tells me back, 'Because of you, Tío Fidel, I was given a really big spanking that day.' Of course it was not because of me. We just tease each other."

I like that I am not the only little girl who gets into trouble.

Pégame, Soy Pecadora

I love raisins. Grama uses pasas in *arroz con leche*. Her sweet rice is creamy and packed with raisins. Raisins are baked into cinnamon rolls and oatmeal cookies. I eat them right out of the box. Grama tries to keep me from eating them by putting them in the trastero on the top shelf. I can't reach the top shelf in the cupboard, except that I have a way of solving all my problems.

Grama keeps potatoes in a small five-gallon wine barrel. The wine barrel is right beside the cupboard. I climb the wine barrel to reach the raisins. I sneak only a few so that she will not find out. I learned this trick a long time ago.

One morning while Grama was out feeding the chickens, I climbed the barrel like I always do, but it was empty and my weight tipped it over. I tumbled to the floor and hit my head on the hard adobe wall. Blood gushed out all over my face and the hand I held to my aching head. I cried and Grama came rushing in. "What have you done?" She looked and said, "You split your head open," and poured sugar on my cut. "You were after the raisins, weren't you?" She picked me up. "When you disobey me, you commit a sin. When people sin they usually get hurt. I have to spank you for disobeying." And she did. First she ministered me, then spanked me. I could not believe it!

I love going fast on my tricycle. I ride all over the yard, over bumps and little arroyos and rocks. Grama has told me hundreds of times not to ride up the driveway because it is too steep. I can't resist and decide to anyway. To my surprise, I tumble and roll. Of course Grama hears my cries and runs to find me wiping gravel off my face, knees, and elbows. She picks me up off the ground and holds me, wiping my tears, and then she spanks me. "One day you will listen. Why must you always disobey? I am only concerned for your safety."

I beg Grama to let me help her wash clothes. She usually sends me out to play or help Grampa with something. She finally says yes and is showing me how to pull on the rope to bring up a pail of water from deep down in the well. I insist that I can do it myself. She rolls her eyes and shakes her head but hands me the rope. The bucket is so full I am nearly pulled into the well with its weight. I cannot hide the fear I feel.

Grama moves her shoulders. "See, you understand why I said no."

She figures I can carry a small *olla de diez*, bucket, filled with water over to the big fifty-five-gallon drums, the ones Grampa set up to heat the water. I carry bucket after bucket to fill those containers and still they are not full. Grampa passes me with two larger buckets and is back a second time before I ever reach the barrels. Finally the two drums are filled with water and Grampa lights a fire under the water containers.

It takes so long for the water to boil. My grandparents finally fill the wringer washer with hot water and the tub for the rinse with more buckets of cold water. A second tub holds the clothes ready to hang.

Grama lets me push the clothes down in the rinse water. I stick my arms in all the way to my sleeves. It cools my elbows off. I want to rinse my face off, but Grama put blue stuff in it. "To make the clothes whiter," she says.

I'm ready to do something more important. "Grama, can I pass clothes through the rollers?" I can tell she is not too sure but gives her okay. I pull a chair over and climb, all the while smiling proudly.

Grama gives her instructions. "Pass the handkerchief through, like this."

"That was easy, Grama. Let me do it by myself."

"Do all the hankies before you try anything else."

That is what I do once, and then again. I'm so sure Grama is happy I am so helpful. Then I feel a tug, a pull. My braid is caught in the roller. "Help!"

Grama hits the machine, which makes the rollers split apart, letting me free. "That's it." She pulls me off the chair. "I warned you not to get so close. Why do I let you talk me into these things? For disobeying my instructions, I have to spank you." With one swift hand my butt gets a good whack. "Go. Go play."

No matter how careful I try to be and to do everything like Grama wants, somehow I can't get it right. Oh well.

Weeks later I am allowed to help with the laundry again. This time my fingers get stuck in the rollers. Grama quickly releases the lever and frees me, but now she does not spank me.

Eloy has turned the old school bus into a getaway. Removing most of the seats has opened it up into a large space. The few seats that remain in the bus work as couches. A single light bulb hangs loosely from some electrical wiring that is woven through a window. No one is permitted to play in the bus unless Eloy gives his OK.

My brothers and sisters and my cousin Lucille come to visit us. My mother and father, Irene and Tomas Tafoya, stopped in Santa Fe for Lucille. I want to show my sisters the neat bus-house, so we sneak in. Eloy is not home anyway.

Lightning and thunder warn us that it is about to rain. We are playing house and don't pay much attention to the weather. It rained earlier in the day before they arrived, and besides, even if it does rain, we are protected in the cozy bus.

One of my sisters hears our mother call for us. "We better go. I think it is time to eat."

Walking to the front of the bus, I feel a pull like something grabbing my leg. It hurts but there is nothing I can see to cause me pain. Dolores follows and I hear her scream. She felt it too. We continue to walk and I feel sharp tingles up my leg. "Ouch!" I jump on a seat and it stops. "Sit here," I say. "It doesn't hurt when I am sitting."

She does not move. "When I move off this rubber pad, I get a shock. I better stay here."

I see fear in Dolores's eyes. This scares me more. Now Grama is also calling. We try to leave the bus but the shocks are stronger. We start screaming for help, but no one hears. Lucille shows up and calls to us from right outside the bus. In the commotion, she decides to climb in. The first step she attempts to take shocks her, so she runs to tell Grampa.

Finally, Grampa comes to the bus. "Get down!" he yells.

I move toward him but after one step I quickly return to my seat. "We can't, Grampa." I cry. "If we move, we get shocked."

He could see that we were not going to go to him. He grabs the bar close to the steps to pull himself up. With one leg in and the other off, he leaps off backward. He tries a second time, this time avoiding the bar, but immediately jumps back. "You stay right where you are. I'll be right back. Don't move, you hear?"

When Grampa leaves, I feel like we will never leave this bus. It feels like a trap. I curl my knees up close to my chest to make sure they do not accidentally touch the floor and drop my face between my knees. I cry, and so do my sisters.

Grampa returns and by now Grama and my mother are with him. "You can get out now," he says. We don't move. We are still afraid. He comes into the bus and shows us that we will be safe. "I disconnected the electricity that Eloy had connected to the bus. You will be okay now."

I do not move. He scoops me up and carries me. Dolores and Diana follow. We all go in to eat, but not without hearing, "I keep telling you not to disobey. It is a sin to disobey and you get hurt every time. You are not to go into that bus again. I hope you listen this time. You have already been told. I have to spank you."

The door to the attic is open. A thought comes to me: *I have never seen the door open before.* I see the ladder leaning on the wall. The wood ladder is old. Exposure to the weather has beaten up the wood. I have seen Grampa and Grama climb it many times. Climbing looks easy. I remember how Julia climbed a ladder in Grampa's story. She was looking for chicos.

As if someone else is controlling them, my hands grip the splintering wood. The first step is hard to reach, but I tiptoe and do it. My hand cannot reach the step and certainly my foot never will. I look around to see what I can do. The *cajete*, a tin tub, that we bathe in is not hanging on the wall but leaning against it. I pull it over, climb on it, and from here I am tall enough to start my ascent to the attic. I am right. It is easy to climb a ladder.

After my eyes adjust to the darkness, I see there are no chicos in this attic, but there are so many other things up here. My tricycle! I had been looking for it. I drag my tricycle closer to the attic door. I look outside and realize how high off the ground I am. The blue sky looks pretty, but now, all of a sudden, I feel afraid. I am thinking about this when I hear Grama.

"What are you doing?" She is yelling at somebody.

I look out and see her standing with her hands on her hips yelling up at the sky. Then I realize it is not the sky she is yelling at; she is yelling up to me. Oh no, I'm thinking, now what?

I have no more time to think about it because she is climbing up the ladder and yelling out to Grampa. "*Ven acá*, Fidel!"

Grama does not come into the attic. She instructs me to turn my back to her and reach for the rung with my leg. I look at her and see Grampa is on his way from the fuerte where he was working. I tell Grama, "I can't see where I am going if I turn around."

Grama raises her voice. "You do not need to see. I'll hold your leg and place your foot on the step. ¡Ándale!"

"But . . ."

She says, "Do as I say. Right now!"

The sky looks so big. The ground looks so far. I want to do as she says, but my knees feel weird. I think they are shaking.

"Give me your hands," Grama demands. "Reach for my hand."

"I can't." My voice breaks and now I am crying.

"*No llores.*" She is getting angry.

I hear Grampa speak. "*Déjala.* Let me talk to her."

Grama climbs down slowly. "You can help her down. She won't even try."

Grampa takes two rungs at a time. "Grab my neck," he says to me.

I see his pleading eyes through my tears.

"You can do it. I can go in there for you, but it is better if you let me carry you from here."

Grama is on the ground, looking up at us both. "What were you doing up there?"

"I was looking for my tricycle," I answer.

Grampa climbs into the attic. I move aside. He grabs the tricycle, hangs half way out of the attic door holding the tricycle, and asks Grama to reach for it. Once she puts it down on the ground, Grampa puts his arm around my waist and pulls me to the attic door. I feel safe in his arms and let him carry me down. When we are about three steps from the ground, he stops. He says, "Put your feet on the rung and hold the one above with your hands."

I do as he asks. I know that I will be able to climb down from here. At the very end I jump down and land on my feet.

As expected, I receive a spanking from Grama. I get spankings when I sin. I wonder why anyone needs a confession after a spanking.

Pollitos y Más Pollitos

A large, noisy box full of chicks and more chicks came in the mail one day. Both Grampa and Grama had to squeeze it past the kitchen door because it hardly fit. Grama could not wait to take a peek. I looked in to see what all the excitement was about and saw the cutest yellow *pollitos* peeping and climbing over each other.

One by one Grama picked them out of the box and put them on the floor next to the stove in a large circular cage Grampa built out of chicken wire. "*Pobrecito*. This poor little thing is sick." She gently placed the sick chick in a separate box.

"What will happen to it?" I asked.

"We'll take special care to feed it with an eye dropper until it gets better."

"Are there any roosters?"

Grama laughed. "It's a little early to tell. Look on the head and sometimes you can tell a *gallito* from the rest, but usually it is only a guess. In a few weeks we'll be able to tell for sure."

Grama counted one hundred total. She separated five to nurse back to health and two came dead. She took one of them and put her hands over its beak and tried to help it breath, but the chick did not respond.

"Who sent us these pollitos?"

Grampa said, "She orders them from the catalogue."

"From Sears catalogue?"

"When we got married and moved to our own house, your grama didn't ask for tables and chairs, or beds and closets; she asked for chickens. 'We need our own chickens,' she said. So she ordered her first hundred chicks. They have always been good not only for us to eat chicken and eggs, but over the years she has sold eggs for extra money."

About ten days later the chicks were able to get out of their caged area. They were driving me crazy with the noise they made all day, especially at feeding time. Grama loved every chick, even if they were stinky and she had to clean up after them. By now I was saying, "I think ducks are cuter. You should buy me a duck."

To my surprise, one day Grampa showed up with a duckling. I loved my duckling. I held it every day and played with it, as though it was a rubber duck. My loving squeeze took the life out of it. "Oh!" I cried. "Oh!"

My grandparents tried to comfort me. "It was an accident, hija."

"But I killed my ducky. Are you sure you can't breath into the beak, Grama? You did that for a chick one time."

"Not possible, hijita. Not this time."

"Oh, Gramita, what am I to do?"

Her hugs and Grampa's hugs were not enough. I felt so awful. Grampa tried to take the duckling out of my hands.

"No! I want to hold it."

"Let me take it, Gloria."

"Where? What will you do with him?"

Grampa did not answer.

In the meantime I knew what was proper and right. "We need to have a funeral."

I gave orders and for the first time they followed my instructions. Grampa found a little box and we put my duckling in it. I chose the place to bury it, and I dug the little hole myself. The three of us formed a single-file procession from the well to the hole. I insisted we sing a song and say a prayer. I even made Grama wear a bandanna on her head. We took turns piling dirt over the little grave, and then with two tied sticks, we made a cross. From all appearances this little grave was beautiful. During all the busyness, I stopped crying without noticing.

Celebraciones

Celebrations like Rita's wedding don't happen enough. Grampa, Grama, and all of Mora eat, dance, and even cry.

This morning we arrive at the church early to watch Rita get out of the station wagon. She sits all by herself because her long white dress fills the whole back seat. Aunt Mary opens the door to help Rita out. All I see are Rita's shoes moving in the air, struggling to touch the ground. One hand reaches for Aunt Mary and the other holds on to the car door as she eases herself out. And finally, the most beautiful white dress I've ever seen is revealed. Aunt Mary pulls here and straightens there. A veil covers Rita's face, but I can see her big smile.

Rita and Uncle Manny crook arms and walk up the aisle. The church is full. Everyone's eyes are on the bride. I realize her hair is short and wonder why she cut it. Rita's eyes are on Juan. He is standing up at the altar waiting for her. It is the first time I have ever seen him. He is a handsome guy. Terry is already at the altar. She is the madrina. I don't know the best man.

Many cars follow the bride and groom to Aunt Mary's house. Cars stop on the road before reaching the driveway. People leave their cars. A violinist and a guitarist play music like a *marcha* and everyone follows the bride and groom in procession all the way to the house. They walk, march, or dance in rhythm to the music. Rita and Juan lead the wedding guests into the house and the music stops and everybody claps.

The house is filled with wedding guests. I walk into the kitchen and am told to go outside and play. I sneak a quick look into the dining room and see Rita sitting next to Juan and Terry and the priest sitting by Aunt Mary and Uncle Manny. There are two tables full of people. The wedding couple, the *padrinos*, and people of respect eat first, and other adults and the children will be fed later. The cooks eat last.

Rita's best friend, Becky, is taking lots of pictures. Grama and Tía Tere

Bernardino home on furlough, circa 1944. Left to right, standing: Fidel, Bernardino, Ninfa, and Irene; sitting: Fidel Jr., Casimiro, and Eloy.

My parents' wedding day, August 31, 1947. Left to right: Patrociñia Sisneros Tafoya, Ninfa Romo Valdez, Irene Valdez (my mother), Tomas Tafoya (my father), Fidel Valdez, and Jesús Tafoya. Photo courtesy of Manuel Tafoya.

are serving food. The men are outside, some smoking and drinking wine. It is exciting to see so many people. They are everywhere. I am playing with my cousins and my brothers and sisters. We are running all over the place. We just left the corral, where we fed the horses some hay, and now Bingo, the shepherd dog, is chasing us.

Bingo is really good at gathering the cows for Uncle Manny at the ranch. He rides on the back of the truck or runs alongside the horse. He always comes when Uncle Manny whistles or calls him. I think Bingo is more helpful than Chulo, our dog, when it comes to ranching.

The wedding moves from Aunt Mary's house to the school gym. Decorations hang from the ceiling from one side to the other. Tables and chairs are set up so the guests can sit. The wedding party walks in beat to the music. Everyone is standing and clapping until the bride and groom sit at the head table next to the table with the wedding cake and the *brindis* table. Another table has presents piled high on it and under it.

The church does not allow dancing during Lent so the band quits playing except the "Marcha." The wedding march ends in a circle around the bride and groom. Men pin dollar bills all over Rita's wedding dress so that they can have a dance with her. The women pin dollar bills on Juan and dance with him. It looks like they are wearing money instead of clothes. I have never seen so much money. My cousins and I make our own circles and dance holding hands, twirling until we get dizzy.

People are calling, "Brindis, brindis!" Ernest, Rita's older brother, gives the first toast to the bride and groom with homemade vinito, capulín wine. Many more good wishes and drinks to the wedding couple are offered. The brindis table is full of bizcochitos, *pastelitos*, chile rellenos, cakes, pop, punch, and coffee. People help themselves to sweets. I help myself to apricot pastelitos and bizcochitos. I think maybe I have eaten too many already because all the twirling is getting me sick.

Rita and Juan open wedding gifts, one after another. Finally it looks like they are about to finish up. A man is walking up to them with his guitar. The whole room gets quiet and everybody stands around the bride and groom while he sings the "Entrega." His words tell a story about Rita and her parents and how she now belongs to Juan, and how much she will be missed at home by her parents and sister. Many people, including Rita, cry. His words offer advice on marriage. People laugh at some of his advice.

It is dark when Grampa finishes helping Uncle Manny pack the truck with the wedding presents and we finally leave the gym. Fun days end so quickly. I can't wait for the next wedding.

I don't remember the drive to Aunt Mary's house because I fell asleep.

Grama says I have a surprise coming. Grampa is driving us into town. We just turned at the church and stop at the convent. I guess we have to talk to the nuns about Viola before I get my surprise. I think she is in trouble again, but I can't see how, because Viola is in Corrales, helping my mother for the summer. Grama, Grampa, and I are waiting at the door for a nun to answer our knock.

Six nuns open the door, Sister Casilda, Sister Melissa, Sister Malachy, and Sister Casianita among them. They stand at the doorway with us. They are holding a cake, frosted in white, with six lit candles on top. The Sisters sing "Happy Birthday" to me! This is the first birthday cake I have ever received. I giggle. This *is* a good surprise.

Sister Malachy's voice trembles softly when she sings. I can barely hear her, and that is only because she is standing right next to me. When they have finished singing, she says to me, "I taught your grandmother when she was in high school, and I also taught your mother when she was in high school."

Sister Casianita says, "My birthday was yesterday, on Saint Ann's Day." She looks to be pretty old too, but Sister Casilda is the oldest.

I say to Sister Casianita, "My middle name is Ann."

She says, "Probably they named you that because you were born one day after the feast of Saint Ann."

The candles continue to burn. Someone says, "Blow out the candles."

Sister Ann nudges me forward. "Make a wish and blow out the candles." My grandparents are smiling and clapping right along with the nuns. All the attention is on me. I can't stop smiling.

Grama is holding the cake. We will eat it at home. I keep turning back and waving good-bye to the women in black. They wave until we drive away.

Grampa parks the truck in front of Maria Sanchez's store. "Ándale," he says. "Get down and see what we find for the birthday girl."

I jump off the truck into his arms and we rush into the store. There are a couple other storefronts on this long white building. "Maria's" is painted in big green letters on the glass door. Through the green wood–framed windows I see a manikin wearing white, holding arms out and upward, with separated slender fingers on dainty hands. She looks like a dancer in a flared skirt that is pulled and pinned to stay. The minute we walk in, Maria greets us. "Fidel and Ninfa, how are you?" Without waiting for an answer she adds, "So good to see you. *Entren, entren. Lleguen.*" We enter and accept her welcome hug.

I leave the store in brand-new white sandals that buckle on the side and new lacy socks. I like having birthday surprises.

Adiós Gramita

I woke up this morning to the scents of coffee and fried eggs. We eat eggs during the week when the chickens are laying well. Chicks have hatched and *culecas*, the brooding hens, are over being so aggressive and now allow us access to the eggs.

Like any other August day, I am playing. I see a green car drive up and run to see who it is. Uncle Fidel gets out of his car. I never call him Fidel, just Uncle Junior. I haven't known him long. He has curly hair and everyone says he looks like Marlon Brando, whoever that is. He recently returned from the navy. He hitchhiked home and surprised Grama. Most of the time he stays in El Alto at Aunt Mary's house.

I follow Junior into the house to see what he is doing here. The car is new and I find out that he bought it with money he saved while in the navy. He calls, "Mama." Grama doesn't answer even though I know she is in the other room. I can see her on the floor next to a suitcase holding one of my dresses.

Uncle Junior sits on the bed next to her. "Is everything ready and packed?"

Grama notices me standing behind him. "Sh," she says, "she is right behind you."

"You haven't told her yet?"

Grama shakes her head. "Come sit by me, hijita." She pulls me onto her lap. I can sense she is sad but I don't know why. "Leave us alone for a while," she tells Junior. I look at him, and then turn to look at her.

I watch Grama cry, holding her face behind her hands until her sobs are loud. Her body shakes, like when she cried at Mina's funeral. I see that in the suitcase she has packed my dresses, socks, and underwear. I stand and put my arms around her. "No llores, Gramita."

Her hands feel my face, then my head, and she keeps looking at me with her sad eyes. She reties the belt on my dress, then pulls my socks up and fixes the fold.

"Why are you crying?"

Kneeling, she pulls me to her and buries her face in my hair. I think that helps because she has stopped crying. "Hijita," she says, "I need to tell you something. Today your tío is taking you to see your mama. She is so happy you are going. I know you will have so much fun with your brothers and sisters."

The suitcase tells me that what she is saying is true. She keeps talking like she can't stop herself. "A long time ago, when you first came to live with us, you were just a little baby learning to walk. Your mama told me then that she wanted you to go live with her when it was time for you to go to school. It is time. When you are six, you start school."

I listen but don't understand. I cry right into Grama's neck and my chest hurts because she is saying I am going away to live. "I have to *live* in Corrales? I want to live here with you and Grampa." I talk, hoping to get her to stop this tumbling feeling in my stomach. "I never want to leave you, Grama. Not even for a day."

Grama knows I'm telling her the truth. She knows I cry when I go stay with Aunt Mary for a night or two. I cry the whole time I am away from her until Aunt Mary gets fed up and brings me back home.

I am drooling all over Grama's neck. She keeps explaining. "Your mama and daddy want you home. They miss you and love you." Gulps of air make her cough. "Hay, hijita." Clearing her throat, she pauses to look at me. "*Mija.*" I can tell she means to send me away. "Choose the dress you want to wear for the trip. You will look pretty for your mama when you get to Corrales."

I have a favorite Sunday dress. She helps me put it on, and when she buckles my new sandals, I run. I run as fast as I can, out of the bedroom, past the middle room, through the kitchen, and out the kitchen door. I hear her calling me, but I keep running. She calls, "Fidel!" I don't look back.

Uncle Junior calls my name and yells, "Get back here!" I don't obey. I don't care if it's a sin. I glance back. He is coming after me.

He is going to have to catch me. I run past the fuerte and past the *quelites* patch, around the place where we pick flowers for May crowning. He is yelling at me to stop. I run past the rock I use for a bed when I pretend to be a sleeping giant. My legs pound the ground toward the rock that forms a bowl to catch my holy water when I play church. I'd make the sign of the cross now if I thought I had time. I skirt the currant bushes hoping to escape. Changing course, I run down the hillside toward the old school bus. Junior and I play cat and mouse until I run to the old gray car that is wasting away on the hill. Tío Adelaido's house has smoke coming from the chimney. If only I could fly like a bird, I could fly there and hide. Junior is very close. I better hurry. Grampa's truck is my only hope. I open the door. My plan is to run out the other door. Junior grabs my leg. I hold the door handle and pull my body away, kicking his hand with my free foot, my body stretched across the truck seat. My hand is losing its grip. I look for something to grab; dirt on the floor and blue sky are all I see. My hand slides onto the gearshift. I hold tight. He holds both my legs and pulls. I can't get away.

Uncle Junior yells, "¡Basta! Enough. That will do."

He carries me into the house, squirming, kicking, and crying. He spanks me and holds me tight, but I keep fighting for my freedom. Suddenly I am gasping for air. Water gags me. Junior has poured the gallon bucket full of cold drinking water over my head. I didn't see it coming. I didn't see any of this coming. I choke and can't breathe.

Junior carries me into the bedroom, holds my arm, and removes my wet clothing. Restrained, I stand before him while another dress goes over my head and is buttoned, the belt tied into a bow. Lifting one leg at a time, dry undies and dry socks slip on. I really don't care about what clothes are going on, but Grama breaks her silence. "Put her new sandals on."

"They're wet," Junior says.

"She wants to wear her new shoes," Grama repeats.

Junior leans me against his leg while buckling my shoes. I can see all that is happening to me but make no effort to stop it. He holds my hand and takes me to Grama. My arms hang at my side and I let Grama embrace and kiss me. She asks for a hug. I can't make myself, so she hugs me hard and kisses me again. She follows us to where Grampa waits in the yard for his good-bye. Grampa stands there looking like he is the one who just about drowned. I run to him. I wrap both arms around his legs. He lifts me up to his face and I see tears flood over the rims of his eyes. He asks, "¿Quién te ama?"

Somehow I smile and say, "Tú."

"¿Porqué?"

"Porque sí."

I hug him so tight and so long that Junior pulls me away. "We have to go."

Grama comes up to me and this time I sink my face into her tummy, my arms clinging to her body. "Glorita." She touches my face. "Adiós, mi hijita."

"Adiós, Gramita."

I leave Las Aguitas in Junior's car. He drives and I sit in the back seat, my chin touching my chest, trying hard to silence my cries until I slip into a deep slumber.

I wake to the sound of a car door. Junior is out of the car. I hear voices and see that Tío is talking to a woman. She closes the door to her house, walks to the car, and climbs in on the driver's side. Tío closes his door and she scoots up close to him. He turns to me. "This is Lorraine. She is going to Albuquerque with us."

She says, "Hello."

I say, "Hello."

Tío looks at her and winks at me. "You can call her Aunt Lorraine."

I say nothing.

"Come on, try it. Say 'Aunt Lorraine.'"

Head tipped downward and eyes looking up at them, I parrot, "Aunt Lorraine."

He turns back to the steering wheel, putting one arm around Lorraine. "We're in Santa Fe and will be in Corrales before you know it."

Lorraine scoots even closer to Tío and we drive off. I doze off again, disappearing from this unwanted ride.

I wake up to see my mother. She is carrying me out of the car. "You're home," she says.

Part II

| *1957–1966* |

Corrales

My short reign as queen is over. I have become a "we" instead of an "I." My many companions where I live with my parents are Dolores, Tony, Diana, and Mark. I have so many playmates that I am rarely alone. And yet I feel lonely. It feels wrong to be here. Dolores and Tony are older than me. Dolores is two years older and knows how to play jacks and jump rope. Tony is exactly one year older and can jump into the ditch and swim to the other side. Diana is almost two years younger than me. Mark will be two in December. I like having sisters and brothers.

Some mornings I wake up thinking I am back at Grama's. It may be a rooster's crow, or the way light at dawn comes into the room, or when fresh morning air touches my face. But there is none of the Spanish music filtering through walls or the familiar quiet mumbling. That is when I remember where I am. Right at that moment of recognition, I feel a prick of sadness right below my chest.

Dad is the ditch rider and checks to make sure the water is flowing smoothly. He clears out tumbleweeds that accumulate under bridges and in culverts and any other debris that can cause a ditch to flood. Mostly it is people who cause floods by damming up the water to irrigate, then forgetting about it. Water rises too quickly and eventually breaks loose, flooding neighbors' yards and roads.

Dad goes in his little red pickup to make his rounds early in the mornings, midday, and at night. There are three ditches in Corrales. At one time, only one existed, according to Dad. He and the locals call it the *acequia madre*, the mother-ditch. "Things are always changing, hijita," he said to me. The way he said it made me think that he doesn't exactly like the fact that change is always happening. I know how he feels. I never wanted to leave my grandparents to come live in Corrales. In fact, maybe my dad can see my sadness. Maybe that is why he brought it up.

Tafoya Corrales chile huerta, alfalfa field, with Sandia Mountains in the background, circa 1970s. Photo courtesy of Gloria Zamora.

I ride with him on his rounds one morning. He lets me get down off the truck and stand close enough to be safe from falling into the ditch. Dad goes on talking about the ditches. "Now the middle ditch is called the Corrales acequia. Corrales Main is the farthest west, and east by the bosque is La Sandoval, also known as the Lateral Ditch."

I like hearing about his work, but mostly I like the way the morning air feels on my face when I ride in the back of the truck. It reminds me of the air in Mora. I am glad he allowed me to come with him.

The truck clanks along over ruts, and every now and then Dad stops the truck to see why the water is breaking up. Even the constant rocking over ruts reminds me of being in the truck with Grama and Grampa.

Climbing out of the truck, I listen to my father speak. "About one hundred and sixty families irrigate from these here ditches. They bring the water from the Rio Grande and that water gives life to alfalfa, corn, and chile fields. Of course apple orchards and all the other fruit trees depend on the water too." He bends, holding the pitchfork up with one hand and with the other almost reverently cups water in his palm. Letting it drain slowly between his fingers, he says, "This is living water. See how chocolate brown it is?"

It looks red to me.

"When it is muddy like this, it means it rained up north. Without the Rio Grande and irrigation ditches there would be no fruit or vegetables growing in this valley."

I had fun today listening to Dad and riding in the fresh air. I'll get used to living here with my mother and father and sisters and brothers. I will.

Dad and Mom just drove off in the truck to go on his evening rounds. I wanted to go too, but they said no. I am so disappointed, I want to be alone. The washroom floor is a good place to be alone. I wish Grama could be here.

There is a strange hissing noise coming from a white tank right in front of me. A blue flame is sparking inside the tank. I can see it through a small opening. Oh my God, it *is* fire. I worry. The house will burn. I better get Dolores.

I run outside where she is playing with Tony and make her follow me into the laundry room. "You see? Can you see that fire?"

"Gloria," she says, shaking her head, "don't worry." She sits on the floor close to where I sat before. She pats the floor with her hand. "Sit here, next to me."

It is my turn to shake my head.

"Let me show you something. Come on, sit by me."

Slowly I lower myself to the floor. She puts her arm around my shoulders. "There is a flame." Her voice is really nice and soft. "That little bit of fire heats water in this big tank."

"Grama heats water in the *pato* or the calentón on the stove."

"That's because she has to. We don't have to. We just turn on the faucet and hot water pours out from this tank into our sinks."

I look at Dolores and think, *She knows so much.*

Taking my hand, she invites me to play outside with her and Tony. "Are you still afraid?" she asks.

"I guess so. A little bit, anyway."

"Well, don't be. That flame is nothing compared to the fire in Grama's stove. Right?"

I know she is right. I follow her outside to play.

School Days

My first day at school, I follow Dolores and join a line in front of the double doors, the entrance to Sandoval Elementary School. Mr. Spring, the principal, stands on the steps leading to the front doors and instructs us to face the flag that flaps in the air high above our heads. I watch and copy what the other kids do. My hand goes over my heart and I listen to the children recite the Pledge of Allegiance. Mr. Spring talks for a few minutes. I don't understand English so I continue to mimic what I see and follow Dolores and the other students into our school.

At the end of a long hall is the gym, and Mr. Spring walks into an office straight across the hall. Each side of the hall is lined with numbered and decorated classrooms.

Dolores takes me by the hand to my room. "Don't be afraid. I'll be over there." She points to room number eight, down the hall. "Go on in," she says. "I have to go to my room; the bell is ringing."

I don't move or let go of her hand.

She pulls her hand away. "Go."

Mrs. McCarthy, my teacher, has us sit. Clay, glue, crayons, and chalk dust are new smells to me. Striped shadows appear on desks, books, and children faces, made from the sun's glow through the window blinds. Even my arms have lines marked across them. I think some of the other faces look confused, just like me. I notice that almost everybody in the room speaks Spanish and maybe only three girls and one boy know English. Still, Mrs. McCarthy speaks in English as if we are going to understand her.

At recess I can't locate Dolores. The steps I sit on are separate from the rest of the school. This building is separate from the other rooms, all by itself, like me. It smells like a kitchen. It feels good to sit in the sun and watch the kids play from here.

Later the lunch bell rings. Students grab their lunches and go outside.

Sandoval Elementary School, now part of Corrales Elementary, circa 1958–1959. Left to right, standing: Ruth Weaver, Susana Maestas, Dolores Tafoya, and Diana Tafoya; sitting: Margaret Armstrong, Gloria Tafoya (myself), Clair Koontz, and unknown. Unknown photographer.

The lunchroom steps are busy, but where else should I go? Kids bump me as they hurry up the steps into the cafeteria.

Dolores comes running up to me. "We have to hurry." She motions for me to follow her. "We are going home to eat lunch. Tony already took off."

We run to a field behind the school. The horse fence has a spot where we can crawl under and not worry about the barbwire on top. Dolores tells me she is afraid of barbwire ever since she cut her leg climbing over a fence. She shows me a scar on the back of her leg. "Keep running," she says.

Mom has beans, tortillas, cucumbers, and chile served in *charolas*. Large bowls of food and plates are set on the table, ready for us to eat. Daddy joins us for lunch too. He is home from his morning rounds.

Tony, Dolores, and I race back to school. We even have a few minutes to play on the swings before the bell rings. "Meet me at the front doors and we'll walk home together," Dolores instructs. "Do you know how to get to your room?"

The first day of school is over. I am waiting for Dolores or Tony. A lot of faces pass me by. There is so much chatter. I am happy when I finally see her. I am not sure she's seen me, until she comes right to me. "Hi, Gloria. My friend Ruth is going to walk with us."

One afternoon a blonde girl joins me on the steps of the cafeteria. She speaks only English and I Spanish. Somehow we have become friends. We play and run with the other children. By the time of our Christmas performance, I have learned plenty of English, thanks to Hildegard. *And* Mrs. McCarthy beats the Spanish out of me by pulling my braids and hitting my head face-first on my desk. I learn pretty quickly to tip my face down into my chest and to use English words.

I am used to napping and fall asleep with my head down on my desk almost every afternoon. I wake to discover the room is empty and follow the sounds to find my way to the playground. Mrs. McCarthy sometimes sits at her desk and teases me: "Well good morning, sleepy head." She is kind about everything except speaking Spanish at school.

I have started playing with everybody, even during class time. Mrs. McCarthy keeps us after school when we cause disruption. We all know the consequences of talking out of turn, so it came as no surprise today when I heard her say, "Gloria, you're talking. Stay after the bell rings." I have no idea what happens when the rest of the kids leave. I sure hope I can go home before it gets dark. I still don't like the dark.

She has me help her erase the blackboard, and then in answer to my prayer, she says, "You can go home now, but remember that we mustn't talk out of turn or when I am talking."

I run fast to make up for lost time. I feel relief when I see Tony and his friend. I tell them, "I'm so glad I caught up with you. Mrs. McCarthy kept me after school."

Tony threatens, "Uh-oh, I'm gonna tell Mom."

"I'll beat you home and she won't believe you," I say desperately.

He races past me and we both stop when we see Dolores. All of us walk into the house together. Tony never does tell Mom anything about me staying after school. I am finding out that my brother is a big tease.

Most days we run home for lunch. Dolores said it is seven-tenths of a mile, if we go the long way around on the paved road. Our shortcut through fields and ditchbanks cuts the trip almost in half. For lunch we always use the shortcut. Sometimes Dolores brings her friends, Ruth, Rebecca, and Margo, to eat lunch. We gobble our food and run back to school before the bell rings.

Tiger, our dog, walks us to school and comes to meet us every day after school. "How does he know when to come?" I asked Tony one afternoon.

"My Tiger is very smart," he answered.

Dolores thinks he can hear the bell ring and runs to meet us. I'm not sure about that because I've seen him waiting at the school gate. Maybe he waits there for hours. Tiger is a sweet dog that never barks at kids or scares them.

On the way home we have to pass by Kaiser, a German shepherd that Estéfan Gonzales and his brother, Ebbi, own. Kaiser growls and shows his teeth and threatens to bite. His owners laugh and say, "Sic 'em." I am always glad when they are not sitting on the steps of their house.

Their house is a long adobe structure that stretches along Corrales Road and bends facing south. Many doors lead to the front yard and the side yard. Each door has two steps leading to it. All doors and long window frames are painted blue. The house is connected to the Tijuana Bar, right across from Perea Hall.

The Gonzales boys are mean, but Fidi, Anita, and the others are nice. Sometimes the girls sit at the doorsteps in their long flare skirts, bobby socks, and oxford shoes, talking and watching the traffic pass by. They are so pretty.

Telephone

The Bureau of Reclamation installed a phone in our house. I want to learn how to use it. The only other person I know with a phone is Grandma Patrocinia.

We have a five-party line. A long ring and two small rings let us know the call is ours. Sometimes after three short rings Diana and I listen in on the other people's conversations. We quietly lift the phone and cover the mouthpiece or the other party will hear our breathing and catch us. If we hear "Wait someone's on the line," we hurry and hang up the receiver. "Get off the line, you nosey blank blanks" makes us laugh so hard we can't stop. Diana thinks she knows one of the voices. I am not positive, but we sure have heard some crazy gossip. We don't even know the people the voices are talking about, but it's funny anyway.

Our phone prefix is diamond. If any other people with diamond prefixes want to call us, they just have to dial the last four numbers. Grandma Patrocinia's prefix is chapel. She lives in Atrisco and does not have a party line. Diana calls her or Aunt Bea almost every day.

Our ringing phone often interrupts dinner. People need to contact Dad for permission to irrigate. Nothing disturbs his mood more than getting a call in the middle of dinner. "Say I'm not home."

It is very hard to tell a lie and I mess up. I'll say, "Just a minute, I'll get him," go in the kitchen, and tell my father the call is for him.

He refuses to take the phone call. "I'm eating. Tell them I'm not home."

"I already said you're home."

"Tell them you made a mistake. Say, I'm sorry I made a mistake, he is not home. May I take a message?"

Dad wants us to be polite and use good manners on the phone, but it feels very impolite to lie. I don't like it, but I do as I am told.

The phone rings for reasons other than permission to irrigate. Women call Dad during the day when their husbands are away at work to rescue a kitten stuck up in a tree, rescue a child who has locked himself in the bath-room, and other such emergencies. He is used to helping people who need to be pulled out when the roads get sandy. Everyone knows he has a tractor.

A second phone has been installed in our house: the fire department phone. It rings at our house and at three other houses. Corrales men volunteer to help put out fires. Each of these men are in charge of calling five other men to give the location of a fire and directions and any other helpful informa-tion. Mom calls the other volunteers while Dad gets ready to go to the fire-house, which is only two blocks from our house. Some men meet at the fire department and leave from there, and others go directly to the fire. When Dad is the first one to arrive, he unlocks the doors and starts preparing the fire truck.

Mom and Dad have rules about the fire phone. "This is not our phone. It belongs to all the people living in Corrales. You will not use this phone for any purpose whatsoever. Understood? In fact, even if it rings, do not answer it. Go call one of us wherever we may be to answer it. If we are not home, let it ring. One of the other volunteers will get it." I don't ever touch that phone.

We share our phone. Our house is always unlocked. In the summer the doors are even left open, be it night or day. If a neighbor needs to use our phone, he or she is welcome to walk right in and use it. Don Juan calls all the way from Utah. Mom yells out across the fields, to our neighbor, in her loudest call, "Vecina, there is a call for you from *el vecino*." When we go to Mora and are gone a few days, the neighbors know they can use the phone or anything else from our house.

Great Discoveries

On Saturdays Mom lets us play all we want, "just as soon as you're done with your chores." We strip the wax off the wood floors, and then wash and wax them again. Mom likes shiny floors. I agree the floors look beautiful after we get them all cleaned up.

The bad thing is that the boys do not help us. We have to do it all. Then they walk into the house with *estiércol* all over their shoes. We fight on Saturdays about that. Dolores scolds, "Tony and Mark, clean those shoes before coming in that door."

Tony argues, "You can't tell me what to do."

She yells, "Mom, Tony is bringing stinking manure in the house again!"

Mom yells from the other room, "Remove those shoes! How many times do I have to tell you?"

Tony mimics quietly, "How many times do I have to tell you," and walks right over to the couch without removing the smelly shoes.

We clean in the morning and play all afternoon until bath time. Mom plays jump rope with us. She turns the rope most of the time and sings the jump rope songs with us: "Spanish Dancer Turn Around," "Cinderella Dressed in Yellow," "Robbers Knocking at My Door," "Sea Shells Cocker Shells," and more songs. Dolores can do "Red Hot Peppers" for a long time. I want to jump rope and play jacks as well as Dolores. We play jacks on the cement steps that lead to our living room. I get better every day.

Diana and I climb trees, like the Chinese elm tree in the backyard. When we climb to the top, the branches sway with our weight. That scares me a little, but I can't let Diana go higher up the tree than me. From up there we can see our school, Mrs. McCarthy's house, the vecina's house, and almost half of Corrales. Diana is a good tree climber, even better than me, but I can't let her believe that. She likes to be better at everything.

My brothers like to play cowboys and Indians. We have plenty of sticks in the yard to use for rifles and bows and arrows. Tony and his friends also play basketball. Tony allows girls to join when his friends go home. I get giggly when Tony tries to take the ball from me. "Here, you can have it!" I exclaim.

"You're no fun," he teases. "What do you think I'm going to do to you? Just play. Try again."

Preparations for Sundays in Corrales are similar to those in Mora. We polish shoes, iron dresses, and take Saturday baths. Only now, warm water pours from a faucet straight into the tub.

Mom walks us to San Ysidro Church for seven o'clock Mass, the only Mass we have. We follow close behind like little chicks following a mother hen. She has not learned to drive, so we walk everywhere or Daddy drives us. No matter what the weather is like, we go to church. After Mass we have catechism in the church, each grade separated by a few pews.

Daddy likes to go to ten o'clock Mass at Nativity of the Virgin Mary in Alameda, because there he doesn't run into people he knows, and they won't ask him if there is water for irrigation.

During the week Dad is willing to help the whole town, but on Sundays he does not want to be bothered about the situation with the irrigation water, especially in a drought year. The Rio Grande can get bone dry. We can dig in the sand and get moisture to build sand castles, but there is no water for irrigation. We can walk across the dry riverbed or cross over to the other side and walk north about two miles and come to the Sandia Pueblo reservation.

To irrigate our fields and garden, Dad pumps water out of the drain ditch and pipes it over to our little irrigation ditch. Other farmers in Corrales have to do that too. The people who do not have pumps will sacrifice their gardens to the sun.

I suppose Dad prefers to pray where he can concentrate. And he probably prays for an end to the dry spell.

We just finished breakfast. Our whole family has piled into the car for a fast ride to visit our grandparents, Patrocinia and Jesús. Diana refuses to move over. I purposely came last so that I could get the space by the window. "Climb over me. You can sit in the middle." She pushes back as I push her.

"I don't like the middle; I'll get car sick," I argue. We continue to push and pull.

"Mom!" she yells.

The minute she calls for Mom, I give up the fight. Diana and I make ugly faces at each other. I climb over her and sit between Mark and Tony. If Mom does not give in to Diana, the brat will cry loudly all the way to Atrisco. Once in Atrisco, she will cry some more so that our grandmother will feel sorry for her.

We race from Corrales to Atrisco on Coors Boulevard, a two-lane road over heart-swallowing dips. Dad gets cheers from us kids, and some loud demands to slow down from Mom. On occasion we meet a car or two going the opposite direction. Dad says it is thirteen miles from our house to Grandma's. There is nothing but sandy hills and sagebrush all along Coors Boulevard. The cottonwood trees that make up the bosque to the east are bright yellow. About half way to Atrisco, a lonely cottonwood sits on the side of the road. Dad says that it makes a good stopping place if people want to have a picnic.

I'm hungry and sneak into the kitchen after giving my grandparents hugs and kisses. Grandma Patrocinia keeps tortillas in a large iron skillet with a tight-fitting lid. We will eat lunch later, but I love her tortillas. A loud clang followed by several more from the spinning lid brings Grandma running to the kitchen. I try to stop the runaway lid but fail.

Grandma laughs when she finds me racing across the kitchen. I look up knowing there is no possible way to deny my guilt. Instead of a lecture about stealing and sinning, to my surprise she smiles. "Do you want butter for your tortilla?"

After eating beans, chile, and tortillas, us kids race to play at the *drenaje*. The drain ditch is behind my grandparent's house. A *cubo* carries irrigation water across the drain ditch. On both sides of the culvert are two four-by-twelve boards used as a bridge. It is a perfect place to play Billy Goat Gruff. We are three billy goats and one gruff, the menacing troll. The troll hangs out under the bridge minding his own business until he hears clippity clop, clippity clop. In a nice voice, I hear him ask, "Who goes there, and where are you going?"

He's so nice, so I answer him in a nice voice: "I am little billy goat Gloria and I am going to town." Gruff's voice changes and he grabs me and drags me into the drain ditch, but not without a fight. I cry for help and no help comes. We take turns at being the troll under the bridge until

Tony starts hitting us with cattails. Before long we are all swinging cattail swords and shooting cattail weapons. The drenaje is more fun than any toy, except for close encounters with its putrid waters and itchy lint off the cattails. Mom does not appreciate our muddy shoes or messy tangled hair.

Going to the Albuquerque Zoo on Sundays is free, so Daddy takes us a few times a year. He buys flat green bean tacos at El Modelo for our picnic. We all stay in the car and wait for him to appear with a package wrapped in white freezer paper.

The drive to the park by the zoo is only a few blocks, but I can't wait to eat the flat corn tortillas fried crisp with a mixture of green beans, cooked tomatoes, and chorizo mounted on top and covered with lettuce and cheese. They smell so good.

If I fail to open my mouth wide enough, half the topping on the tostada falls to my lap. It is so tasty I will pick it up with my fingers to save it and put it back into my mouth.

Daddy makes sure we clean up after ourselves, not leaving a single little bit of trash on the grass. He is a stickler about littering. We hear the same lecture at every picnic we have. "Pick up your trash. No one wants to see garbage everywhere. *We* are *not* litterbugs."

Skipping and jumping and running ahead of our parents, we reach the zoo entrance and wait for them. They walk slowly but can't keep us from running to each exhibit. Monkeys swing back and forth behind cages made out of horse fence and chicken wire. Elephants take slow heavy strides, looking up at us with wrinkly heavy-lidded eyes, and reach for alfalfa with their long trunks. A large alligator lies in the hot sun, almost motionless except to snap at an occasional invisible fly. Much later, we beg to stay longer, but Mom says the zoo is closing for the day.

We have cousins who live in the city and come visit us. Corrales is the country to them. We play baseball, hide and seek, red rover, and zoo. I play tour guide and show them our zoo animals: cows, calves, giant hogs, chickens, and horses. Our dog, Tiger, follows like he is in charge of protecting us. We climb apple trees and play. Daddy takes the older boys fishing. Their mother Julia and my mother are first cousins. They sit in the house talking and making lunch, and later, dinner.

Dad loves to get as far away from Corrales as he can on Sundays. We drive all over New Mexico. He does not concern himself with details like having gasoline in the car, where or what we will eat, or where we will be going. We get in the car and he drives. When he gets there, we know our destination for the day.

We visit the Pueblos, if they are open. We are familiar with the national parks and monuments. Echo Canyon is a favorite stop. We scream, hoot, and sing, taking moments to listen for the echo to answer us multiple times.

Dad loves his state and its history. These trips are opportunities for him to teach and teach some more.

Abó is south of Albuquerque and east of Mountainair. Daddy gives us some history about our state and our grandparents on the drive to Abó every time we go: "Belen was the *fríjol* capital of the world in the thirties. I used to see *sacos* of beans piled on the train cars. Those trains took frijoles to California, Texas, Colorado, and who knows where else."

We drive and drive. Between Bernardo and Abó on highway 60, and east of La Joya, Dad points at a *sierra*. "Look over there. That is Cerro Turu TuTu. That's what Papá said I called it when I was a kid."

It sounds so funny, we all want to say it, so he repeats the words in a childlike singsong voice. All of us try to imitate, even the sound of his voice, and say "Cerro Turu TuTu" several times between laughs.

Dad's Growing-Up Stories

Listening to my father tell story after story is like listening to my grandfather in Mora. He usually starts telling stories when we are on our way to Abó to visit relatives or when we are sitting around the dinner table at night. He and Mom ask us about our days at school and something reminds him about when he was growing up. I like to listen and often have to ask questions. He talks about people he knows. My brothers and sisters usually know who he is talking about, but because I have been in Mora, I am not familiar with them. Dad tells stories about his father and mother and their parents all the time. He loved his grandparents. When I hear him talk about them, I feel connected to them even though they are already dead.

Every time we climb in the car there is some negotiation about where to sit. Mom finally made a rule. Dolores, being the oldest, gets to sit up front with her and Dad. Usually Tony gets the window seat behind Dad, and I get the window seat on the passenger side. The others get to sit in-between. It doesn't always work like this because of conflict and the need to separate those who are fighting. Once we are settled and seated in our assigned places, our trip takes on a happy note. Dad leads into this song: "I'm going to leave"; we echo, "I'm going to leave"; he sings the next phrase, "To Texas now"; and we repeat, "To Texas now." Phrase by phrase we sing, "Ain't got no use, for the long-horned cow." We know the words to "Oh My Darling Clementine." We always sing "Row, Row, Row, Your Boat" in rounds. It gets confusing and crazy and fun all at once. We congratulate ourselves when we end nicely.

About an hour into our trip, Dad starts talking about the past. "Papá was born in La Joya. His parents lost their land when American law came to New Mexico."

I have heard this story before, but each time I hear it he seems to add more.

Juaquín Sisneros, my paternal great-grandfather, and family, circa 1900. Left to right: Trinidad (Tafoya) Sisneros holding Vivianita, Juanita, Esquipula (standing), Federico (sitting), Patrociñia, and Juaquín holding Josefa. Unknown photographer, courtesy of Martin Sisneros.

"Old-timers were used to Spanish law. Lands were granted to the early families so that they would settle in New Mexico. No one paid taxes. Then when Mexico came into power, the Mexican government continued to give land grants to encourage settlement in New Mexico. And still no one was required to pay taxes. When the new American government took over New Mexico Territory, the people had no idea they were now obligated to pay taxes. Either they were not informed or did not know how to read or something."

I interrupt to ask, "You mean even the adults didn't know how to read?"

My father is quick to defend his ancestors. "There were those who were literate but may not have known how to read law, especially if it was written in English. And you have to understand that there were people who had no opportunity to get an education."

By the tone of my father's voice I can tell my question bothered him. I decide not to question him any further. I am surprised, though, that school is not available to everybody.

Jesús Tafoya, my paternal grandfather, with parents Barbarita Apodaca and Antonio Tafoya, circa 1890–1891. Photo from family collection.

Members of the Tafoya family, circa 1924. Left to right, back row: Hildo Esquivel, Tomas Tafoya (my father), and Manuel Tafoya; front row: Antonio Tafoya, Barbara Esquivel, Federico Tafoya, and Lillian Tafoya. Unknown photographer, photo from family collection.

"Anyway," Dad continues, "people everywhere lost their land for back taxes and the *sinvergüenza* rich and shameless gringo lawyers took advantage and bought large tracts of land for next to nothing."

Every time we drive by La Joya, Dad tells of this tragic event. He usually adds, "That's why it is so important to go to school. With an education, people can't take advantage of you."

Heading south toward Socorro, he points at the scenic Manzano Mountains to the west and at the Magdalena Mountains farther south. "See that peak over there? It is called Ladrón Peak. Grandpa Jesús took care of his father's sheep all over those mountains. My grandmother, Barbarita, died when he was twelve years old and left three children behind: my Dad, Tía Lucinda, and Tía Catalina. Catalina was only seven."

I could not believe what I heard. "Dad, do you mean to say Grandpa was only twelve and he had to leave home?" I knew I would be very afraid to sleep out in these mountains at night without shelter. I wondered what he ate, who cooked for him?

"That's exactly what happened," my father emphasized. "I guess my grandfather, Antonio, had no one to take care of his daughters, so he sent my dad to take care of the sheep. He was only a few years older than you, Tony."

I see a few mountain peaks and am unsure which peak Dad is referring to. But I imagine the hills and vast land filled with white dots of sheep and a young boy holding a long stick herding them. I think of the book *Heidi* that my teacher has been reading to us in school. Peter is an eleven-year-old boy who herds goats. He and Heidi become good friends. They spend their days on the green slopes, climbing the peaks of the Swiss mountains. I can place Grandpa Jesús in the story. I have to ask, "Were there wolves and bears and coyotes?"

"Sure, hija. It was his job to protect the sheep from the coyotes and wolves."

"Sounds dangerous to me," I say.

My father looks far into the mountains west of the interstate. He is quiet for a while. "Papá had a lonely life at camp. There was a *campero* named Juanito; he was Papá's primo. This campero died at camp and Papá had to go all the way to La Joya to report Juanito's death. On the way back, they brought a coroner and six people. For testimony of death, to prove it was not murder. This incident happened when Papá was very young."

I am sure Grandpa Jesús was very brave. Traveling all alone through the plains and mountains is not something I ever want to try.

Dad interrupts my thoughts. "There were different camps. Luís Esquibel, who had also lost his mother, and Papá were cousins. Sometimes the two camps would meet. Casimiro, another sheepherder, was hired by Grandpa Antonio to help Papá herd. Once in a while Casimiro would take his earnings, go to Mountainair, and blow his money. One time he bought a silk shirt. He came back saying, '*Ya no hay algodón, nomás pura seda*,' touching the front of his shirt." As my father tells the story, he too touches the front of his shirt. Dad adds, "I guess he wore the silk shirt to dances on Saturday nights."

The story makes me think of *Bonanza* on television. I want to hear more. Listening to Dad's voice is like listening to story time at school.

He continues, "When Tío Melcadez died of cancer, Papá was made administrator of his estate. This was in Contreras, also known as Rancho de La Joya. Papá, having no education, added two hundred and fifty head of sheep to satisfy debtors for Lucinda and Melcadez."

"Who is Melcadez?" Mom asks. "I've heard the name before."

My father answers, "He was Tía Lucinda's husband. They were only married a short time before he died. She was left a *viuda* very young and had to work for other people, cleaning houses and ironing. She did a good job of supporting herself and her two children, but I guess Melcadez left some debts behind."

Driving on, we reach Scholle. The whole area is full of memories for Dad. Listening to his memories is like reading a book. The only difference is that the characters are our relatives. I don't think he can stop telling the story of his relatives. It is very important to him.

Sometimes with my brothers and sisters playing in the back seat, I have a hard time hearing my father. I want him to tell them to be quiet but he doesn't; he just keeps talking to my mother and Dolores. He knows they can hear him.

I pull myself forward and grab hold of the front seat. By leaning my head on Mom's head I can hear what he is saying. "When we moved to Albuquerque, Papá worked for the railroad, and that meant we had passes on the train. We used to come see my grandma in Abó. The train station was right here in Scholle. Someone would meet us here and take us the rest of the way, three miles or so. Sometimes we had to walk to Abó, suitcases and all."

Tony calls out from behind me, "Tell us what happened that time the arroyo flooded."

I didn't think Tony was listening. He was fidgeting and moving and playing with the others.

My dad looks at Tony in the rearview mirror and smiles. "Well, son, it was when Mamá was going to have one of my sisters or my brother Fred. She used to come to Abó to have her babies and to stay for the forty days after. I was too young to drive, but Mamá asked me to drive her. I guess no one was available to pick her up in Scholle."

"Tell about the arroyo, Dad," Tony encourages.

My father laughs at Tony. "You know the story."

Tony says, "Yeah, but tell it again."

"Like I said—" Dad smiles—"I was not the best driver. In fact, I only drove to obey my mother. I think Papá stayed home. When we arrived in Abó, it was raining cats and dogs. I could hardly see where I was going. I drove slowly because my little sisters and mother were afraid. I stopped at the arroyo because the water was rumbling past and really high. You know, deep."

"Was there a bridge?" I ask.

My father shakes his head. "There was never a bridge there, but we could cross the arroyo in our trucks. But this storm was washing everything downriver. My mother and I put boards to try and cross. The water took the boards. There was Mamá all *enferma*, ready to give birth soon, and I didn't know what to do. She and I were soaked and cold. She said to me, 'You can make it across, *mijo*. Give it a try.'"

My dad laughs mischievously. "We climbed into the *troquita* and I drove into the arroyo. At first the water started to take us with it, but by some *milagro* we came to a spot and the tires took hold and we made it across to the other side."

"It sure was a miracle. I love that story," Tony says, patting my father's head. "You sure learned how to drive that day, huh?"

"Yep, son, I sure did. I was scared to death, but what else could we do?"

We make a turn onto the road that leads to where Dad's aunts and uncles live. The first house we see on our left is where Tonito, his cousin, lives. We will stop to visit him on our way out. Antonio and Aurora are my *padrinos*. I have been told several times that I am like my godparents. I am shy like Antonio, my godfather, and at the same time I am friendly and talkative like Aurora, my godmother.

"The first house we'll see is Tío Esquipula's house," Dad informs us. This leads into a tale about his uncle. "Tío Pula was the first one in Abó to get a Model T. He and I went for a little ride in it to get some wood. It had no headlights, or else they weren't working. Dusk came and it was hard to see. We rarely met up with any other vehicles, but this one time on this curvy hill, between Mountainair and Abó, when we reached the top of the hill, we saw some headlights. It was another Model T. We swerved to miss hitting the guy and lost control. We ended up at the bottom of the hill in a small ravine. Boy, that was a close call!"

Dad's laugh always has a mischievous tone when he tells about close calls. We have been told that the house we will stop at first is the house where Grandma Patrocinia was born. "She grew up in that house and later on had her first children there. Manuel, then Tony and me, Lilly, then Fred." Dad has pride in his voice when he talks about *la casita* and his experiences in Abó. "When I was a boy, I came to stay with my grandmother in the summers. Naná La Lá is the name I gave her when I was a child and could not say Grandma Trinidad. She had a large *cajón* for storing all the goodies for winter. One time, when I was maybe eight or nine, I took some apples from the storage box and buried them in the ground in a gunnysack. I planned to eat them later, except the pig escaped from the *trochil* and dug them up. The damn pig gave me away. Oh boy, I was in big trouble."

One story leads to another; it is like he is a boy again. Even his voice changes as he continues, "Because I played hooky so much, my parents sent me to Abó to live with Naná La Lá for a year. I finished eighth grade here. It was a one-room school, first through eighth grade. The teacher, Nicolas Contreras, and most of the students were my cousins. He made sure I learned. He was a good teacher."

I cannot believe my own father played hooky. He's got everybody else's attention now too. The car is quiet as we listen to more of his childhood tale. "I guess I always knew that my cousins in Abó looked up to me. I was from the big city, Albuquerque. They thought I was pretty cool. One summer I told them all that I was in a gang. I told them that if they wanted to be a part of my gang, they had to shave their heads. They all did. When it was my turn to be under the clippers, I said, 'Not me. I'm not shaving my head. Do you think I'm stupid?'"

"Were you really in a gang?" Tony asks.

Dad laughs. "Never. Are you kidding? Now me and my primos can all have a good laugh over those days."

I think Dad was very mischievous. We would get into big trouble if we tried pulling a trick like that on our cousins. At least I think we would. Tony will try. I know he will.

Tío Federico and Dad don't mind that I follow them around the acres and acres they stroll. Dad taps Tío on the elbow. "I remember walking all over the property." He points south. "The *pinturas* and the ruins is where we liked to play."

"Will we go there today?" I ask.

"It's a little walk south of here. Are you sure you want to walk?"

"I want to see the Indian rock paintings you told us about."

Tío Federico is old but he likes to walk. In fact, he walks all over this land every day. At least that is what he tells me. "I take care of our land and make sure nobody throws trash here or comes here for drunken parties." As we begin our climb, we turn to see the spring and the houses below.

Tío points at a fenced-in area to the right of la casita. "We grow corn, chile, and squash. Right over there, hija." He points to a dry weedy portion of sandy sloping land. The fenced-in area gives me an idea of where he is pointing. "Where is the ditch? I can sort of make out the rows."

"We dam up the spring to irrigate the garden. There's plenty of water most of the time, but there used to be a lot more. We used to grow a lot more. When I was a kid, the long rows curved and followed the slopes using the most level areas possible. It was impossible to level at this altitude. We did well and had plenty of frijoles and vegetables for raising a *familia*."

"Altitude here is six thousand feet," Dad adds. "There is rock and clay and sandy soil and still my grampa and my tíos grew good crops. Much more than they do now. I helped every summer when I came to stay. I enjoyed my summers playing with cousins. We grew up more like brothers and sisters."

Pointing to a smaller squared-off area, fenced and to the left of the vegetable garden, Dad smiles. "Naná La Lá grew her tobacco right there. Tobacco or *punche lo que sea*, whatever you want to call it. It had large green, green leaves. It was the water. The spring provided a good life here, for farming and drinking."

Tío Federico nods, his thin lips stretching in a smile. "You listen to your daddy, hija. He tells our story and one day you can tell our story."

My father reaches into his shirt pocket. "*¿Cigarito?*" he asks. Tío shakes his head. Dad stops walking, takes a match out of his pocket, and swipes it against his leg. Cuffing the small flame, he puffs at his cigarette, then slowly walks forward. "I was only twelve when I started smoking. Naná La Lá would send me to get the finest *hojas de maíz* to make her cigaritos. She rolled them really thin and tight, smoked half a cigarette, lit a new one with the first, and then threw the old one away. I would sneak the cigarette stub and smoke it. They had to be the softest, thinnest corn leaves. You could almost see through them."

My mother did not smoke and neither of my grandmothers smoked. I assumed women did not smoke because in all my life, I had only seen men smoke.

Daddy added, "The Santa Fe railroad bought water from Naná La Lá after my grandfather died. They piped it all the way to Scholle. They needed pure water for the engine boilers."

We kept climbing until we reached the ridge. From here the Manzano Mountains and Los Pinos Range were a dark shade of blue, like the blue of darkness in early evening. I'm ready to ask the question Dad hates, are we almost there? In my hesitation, he speaks. "We just have a little more to go. The rest is easier because we are already at the top and we don't have to climb down the other side. We just need to walk south on the ridge to get to the pinturas."

We're inside an overhang of large stone. At least a hundred swallow nests made of mud with small round holes for openings hang on to the ledge as though they are glued. I wonder why they don't fall off.

The rock paintings are so clear. "There are red and black hands painted on the rock. One of these has only four fingers—the middle finger is a stub," I say excitedly. "Look, a figure in black and white stripes resembles a jester in fairy tale books."

Dad points out a red stick woman with a headdress formed like the zia symbol. It appears as though a piece of the rock is broken off. A windmill is carved out of the rock and painted along with other figures and symbols.

I point here and then I point there. I move quickly from one end of the cave to the other. "What is that gold, red, and black figure?" I ask.

"Looks like a king to me."

It is truly a wonderful place. "Ooh, there's a maiden walking with a pot over her head. And two red centipedes crawling over to a blue and red striped flag."

"Ooh," Dad teases.

Tío Federico is happy we are here. "They were once much brighter. The colors fade more and more every year. Can you see the Indian warrior? His gold arms are on his hips and he is wearing black pants. Can you see? His legs are bent like he is doing a war dance."

"Yes!" I answer. "He is wearing a crown on his head."

"I think they're fanned feathers," Dad says.

"Anyway, he is facing another dancer with a blue face and red hair also wearing a gold shirt and black pants. This is so cool!"

My dad says, "Do you suppose that next to him is the chief crowned in long red feathers?"

"Sure, I think so!" My neck is bent as far back as possible, my head tilted upward to the point of almost falling out of balance. A book, a turkey, a rainbow, and so many other wonderful figures are painted on the rock. "I think the Indians were telling a story, but I have to think about it."

Both my father and Tío Federico laugh heartily.

We cross the spring that runs in front of Naná La Lá's home. Tío Federico and Tía Lupe live there now. I like to take off my shoes and sit on the red flagstone and let cool water run through my toes. I have not seen the water very high, but I have heard that when it rains the water level climbs, and in the old days it rose nearly to the kitchen door. Tía Lupe calls us in to eat lunch. I can smell the tortillas and can't wait to *dig in*, as Daddy always says.

During lunch Dad tells about being sent to the salt lakes to bring salt for Naná La Lá. "She used it for cooking and kept it by the stove in a small jar. She would break it into small pieces and it would dissolve in the beans or meat. That was one of my jobs when I stayed here."

I imagine Naná La Lá looked like all the women we come to visit. Maybe she wore black tápalos draped over her head and shoulders. Curious about it, I ask, "Why do all the women dress in black and wear those heavy shawls? They look like little short nuns to me."

Dad scowls. I know instantly I should have kept my mouth shut. I am embarrassed especially because I sit right across the table from Tío Federico.

Dad does not let it go. "These are my aunts. I love them very much and will not tolerate you making fun of them."

"I'm sorry, Dad. I don't mean any disrespect. They do remind me of the nuns in Mora. Why do they dress in black?"

Tío Federico comes to my rescue. "Maybe I can explain. The women are in mourning. It is proper to mourn for a whole year. In large families like ours, there are a lot of deaths, so they dress in black, more than any of us would like to see."

My father repeats, "Much more than we would like to see. But on the other hand, I suppose they are holy, like nuns. They pray all the time. All my life my aunts and uncles have held velorios in their houses for every imaginable saint. Tío Pula and Tía Kika have a velorio for San Pedro, Tío Federico and Tía Lupe honor San Ysidro, Tía Josefita and Tío Luís for San Jose, Tía Vivianíta and Tío Martín for San Pablo, and Tía Juanita and Tío Ramón for San Ramón."

I have attended velorios for dead people, but my relatives in Mora did not have vigils for the saints. I wondered if they put up a coffin or how it was done.

Dolores asks for more beans and in the same breath, "You mean a rosary, like when somebody dies?"

"Exactly like that," Tío Federico answers. "On the saint's day we go to that house and pray the rosary three times. We sing hymns and remember those who have died. If possible, if a priest is visiting, we have a Mass. At midnight we eat from all the food that everybody cooks. It is a feast!"

I am grateful to Dolores for having asked the question.

Tía Lupe adds, "We still have velorios. Come in March, *el día de San Jose.*"

My father is grateful for the invitation. "We'll see, Tía. The irrigation waters open the first of March, and March winds bring more tumbleweeds than you can count. We'll see."

To me, Abó is spending a whole day visiting our aged aunts and uncles, my grandmother Patrocinia's brothers and sisters. It is hard for me to keep their names straight. Dad tries to help, but I can't remember them like Diana does. When Diana lived with Grandma Patrocinia, Aunt Bea brought them to Abó often, and the tíos visited Grandma and Grandpa in Atrisco too.

In Abó everyone lives in little rock houses held together with mud and *enjarradas* with a mud plaster. The doors are short and the windows are small. It is almost dark inside the thick walls. The little houses spread all over their birth-land, turning Great-grandmother Trinidad and Great-grandfather Joaquín's farm into a small village. Grandma Patrocinia moved to Albuquerque when Dad was about four years old. She is the only one who left.

During the long afternoon hours while adults visit and talk, my sisters, brothers, and I get to play in the spring and in the mission ruins. Though we have been told many times not to climb the walls, we climb over and under the walls of the mission church. We run in and out of the many rooms and play hide and seek. Tony and our cousin Mike climb all the way up to the bell tower. Mike tells us that spirits exist in the ruins. We walk the grounds searching for arrowheads and pottery pieces.

We leave the ruins and Abó with filled pockets. Our treasures, dear to us because we are told they are ancient and wonderful, will be put away in a safe place when we get home.

Spring

For Easter, Christmas, and the start of school, Mom puts us on the city bus and we all go downtown. Mom rides this bus to work during the week, but for these outings we all wait at the end of our road by all the mailboxes.

Today she's wearing a hat, gloves, and lipstick. It looks like she is going to work or to church. She has the prettiest smile and the lipstick makes it even prettier. Other times she has taken all of my brothers and sisters, but today only us girls wait anxiously for the bus to arrive.

"Stay together. I don't want to be hunting you down all day," Mom insists.

I don't want to get lost! Besides, helping each other choose new dresses is exciting. We are allowed one dress each, and we get to pick our shoes this time. Our school shoes are selected by Mom. "No, no patent leather. Saddle oxfords are more durable than those shiny glossy things, and they will last the year," she says.

We come out of stores with several bags each and have to be careful not to set them down or lose them. Downtown sidewalks are full of people rushing around and looking into store windows. It feels like a fiesta. McClellan's or Woolworth's is our treat stop. Finding a place for all of us to sit together is not easy. McClellan's is crowded. Mom sends us ahead of her while she pays. "Put your bags under your feet. Make sure you don't leave those bags alone," she says.

I really like the bear claws from Woolworth's, but today I'll be happy with a soda or an ice cream cone. Catching the bus home means waiting. We wait for the right bus and we hold our bags. We are not allowed to open or look inside them while we wait. Finally we are on our way home. "Sit close to me," Mom says.

We fill a whole pew at church. We prance around feeling so pretty in our

Dolores's First Holy Communion, 1957. Front row, left to right: Mark, Dolores, Diana, and Gloria; back row: Tony, Irene, and Tomas Tafoya. Photo courtesy of Beatrice Tafoya.

new dresses, petticoats, lacy socks, new shiny shoes, and Easter bonnets. We even wear new white gloves.

A few hours after Mass, aunts, cousins, and my grandparents from Atrisco finally get to our house. We have a picnic under the elm tree in the backyard and wait for the egg hunt. Dozens of hard-boiled eggs everyone colored the night before are hidden in the two acres south of the house. My aunt's kids are young, so their mamas help them find eggs. Tony, Dolores,

Joseph, Mark, and Tony, 1958. Photo courtesy of Irene Tafoya.

Easter, 1963. Along with first cousins, Edwina Tafoya, my sister, is on the very top row, second from left, in the dress with a large white collar, and Joseph Tafoya, my brother, is in the top row, seventh from left, in a striped shirt. Photo courtesy of Irene Tafoya.

Edwina and my father, Tomas, 1964. Photo courtesy of Irene
Tafoya.

and I rush across the field and start filling our baskets. Tony throws out the
green grass and leaves it for the wind to carry away.

After the hunt we count to see who has the most eggs and that person gets a prize: a kite or a dollar or something exciting. We eat plenty of
candy eggs, chocolate candy, and colored eggs, enough to feel really sick
that night.

Memorial Day marks the end of the school year. The last day of school we
go only for a few minutes, long enough to get the news. We race to collect

the report card that tells whether we pass or fail. I run toward Mom, waving the envelope with a piece of cardboard and hollering louder than the rest, "I passed! I passed!"

A Memorial Day picnic under a cottonwood tree is a perfect way to celebrate the end of school and passing to second grade. Mom packs baked chicken, bread, and potato salad in a box. She brings plates, forks, salt, and a tablecloth to spread over the dirt.

Dolores, Mom, and Dad will not get into the cold water, but the rest of us swim and splash. It is the first picnic after Easter and our first swim of the summer. We won't return to school until after Labor Day.

The Greyhound Bus

Sometimes both Grama Ninfa and Grampa Fidel come for me in the yellow Chevy or the pickup truck to take me to Las Aguitas. Grampa travels at a great speed of forty-five miles per hour. Other cars and trucks zoom past us.

Other times Grama comes on a Greyhound bus or we return to Mora on a bus. No bus station in sight, a suitcase in hand, standing on the side of the road, we wait to be picked up by Greyhound on Second Street. I don't know if the spot we pick to stand is a bus stop, but we stand and when the bus stops, we get in.

My greeting when we arrive in Las Aguitas is Grampa singing, "*Qué bueno, Qué Bueno Que Se Acabo la Escuela.*" It is a song on the radio. We all agree that it is good that school finished for the year and I can come stay with my grandparents for the summer.

My two-month stay with my grandparents in Las Aguitas feels short. We have our own picnics and go swimming too. Work is more like play, because I get to be with Grama and Grampa. We continue to do as we always have. I am very happy to be back home.

I ask Grama, "Is it okay if I still call your house my house?"

Grama says, "This will always be your home, mi hijita."

This morning way before the sun appears we load the car with our luggage. Grampa and Grama are driving me back to Corrales. I am not ready to return, but when I said something about it to Grama, she just shook her head and said, "Hay, hijita, you have to go back. You have to go to school."

The rooster has not crowed. It is early. Silhouette impressions of the mountains press against the sky and the stars hang above the mountains waiting for dawn. Me, I love the quiet and the way everything is colored in dark blue.

Grampa just says, "We might see the sun come up in Santa Fe if we get going now."

Grama says in return, "Let's go."

Kindred Spirits

Kathy stands on short chubby legs by her house in her pretty dress and lacy little socks, wearing a bracelet, ring, and earrings, and waits for me. Her curls flop loosely around her round face. Her small smiling eyes slant as if she is of Asian persuasion. Today is a school day. We walk together every day.

Kathy's mother waits with her. Rosemary is pretty, wears the latest fashions and heavy perfume, and dyes her hair red. She loves Paul Anka and listens to his album so many times that Kathy and I have memorized the words to "Put Your Head on My Shoulders" and "Diana." Rosemary makes certain Kathy always looks neat and curls Kathy's hair every night.

Wisps of hair loosed from my braids, not ten minutes from the time Mom braided them this morning, fly around my oval face. My shoes suck my socks all the way to my toes and I wrestle with the ties on my dress. I don't know how Kathy stays neat all day.

Kathy and I are constant companions. We make up songs and sing all the way to and from school. My dog, Tiger, follows close by. Alongside the paved road we find many treasures like unusual rocks, pennies, or pieces of pretty glass. We skip or play kick the can, always watchful of the traffic.

Coca-cola bottles are treasures we actually hunt for. If lucky enough to find one, we hide it in the weeds close to the school gate. When the bell rings sending excited children home, we retrieve our bottle, cross the street, and walk to Earl's little store. Plenty of kids are hanging out, drinking a soda, or buying a candy, creating happy noise, in no rush to get home. The dust on wood floors mixes with the distinct scent of newly butchered beef, chocolate candy, and all flavors of soda pop. Two aisles of candy-filled shelves make the choices for the after-school crowd irresistible. The bottle will buy us four penny-candies.

Robert, Kathy's older brother, is my brother's friend. Tony and Robert always have Coke bottles for trade. They sneak into people's garage stashes or backyards looking for bottles. They are regulars at the little store. They both share candy with everyone.

Earl knows each and every parent and threatens to tell if anyone causes trouble. Most kids behave in his store, or he literally grabs them by the ear or arm and throws them out.

Mom has us bring bread, potatoes, or some other food when we need it at home. Earl puts it on the tab. The tab runs until the end of the month when Mom pays the bill in full.

One day Diana and I were way at the tiptop of our favorite tree. Tony, Robert, and their friends, Joe and Ray, had been playing basketball and decided to rest in the shade. I don't think the guys knew we were up in the tree. The way Joe was laughing peaked our interest. Diana and I put our fingers to our lips at the very same time, which almost made us laugh out loud, but we laugh silently in order to hear what was about to be said.

"Man," Joe said, "Earl set me up."

Tony shook his head. "No way, man. When? How?"

Joe wiped his forehead with his fist. "You know how we pay for one soda and get two or three and stand there drinking. Well, I think he's onto us."

"Spit it out, man. What are you talking about?" Tony asked.

"Today I saw two quarters sitting on the counter. They were just there. I looked around and nobody picked them up. *Tú sabes.* I took my time to make sure, you know, that they didn't belong to nobody, then I took 'em."

"*¡Sanamagón!* Did that sucker see you take 'em?"

"No. I waited till he was busy in the back. But then I bought one of those strawberry suckers. I picked a lucky one and got a free sucker. I unwrapped it and started licking."

"Ándale, Joe." Tony shoved him playfully. "What about the quarters?"

Joe nearly fell over a tree root trying to get away from Tony. Diana giggled and I wanted to laugh too, but I held it in and shushed her with a stern look and my forefinger hitting my lips. I thought sure the guys below had heard Diana, but Joe was laughing, and the others teasing and shoving at each other kept us from being discovered.

Joe continued where he left off. "When I went up to the counter to pay for the sucker, I gave him a quarter. He looked at me real serious and straight in the eye."

"Yeah," Ray urged.

"His voice got real mean when he says to me, 'Where did you get that quarter?' I started to sweat it, but I looked at him and said, 'My old man gave it to me.'"

"Damn!" Tony said. "Did he buy it?"

"That's when he tells me, 'Well, I put two quarters right here and they are gone now. You know anything about them?' Man, I shook my head real hard. I said, 'No sir, Mr. Works. I don't know nothing about any quarters.' Then I took off and ran all the way home."

"¡Híjole! And he just let you go?" Robert asked.

"I wish! Five minutes later he was at my house. He got in his car and drove to my house." Joe laughed. "By then I was under the bed. Hiding."

"No! Then what, *ese?*"

"He told my mother that I took the quarters and then he left. She looked for me, but I was making sure he was gone before I came out of there."

"Did you get *fregasos?*"

"You know it, man. My mom gave me the belt and left some welts, man. I'll tell you what, I'm not ever gonna steal from that guy again. He's sneaky. I know he knows about the sodas, man. No more sneaking sodas for me."

They went back to playing basketball and I could hear Joe and Tony brag to Ray and Robert that they could beat their pants off any day. Diana and I snuck our way back into the house. Once out of earshot, we did not hold back our laughter.

Kathy and I live on the same street on the same side of the road separated by two fields, a house, and an outhouse. We have just walked home from school. She is asking Rosemary, "Can I go to Gloria's to play for a while?"

"You *may* go for half an hour."

We skip over to my house and play all sorts of things. Pretending to be dancers, we prance on the flatbed trailer Dad uses to bring in the bales of alfalfa. We like the small foreign car parked right under the kitchen window. It is new, just arrived today. Mom said Dad traded something for it. Only one grown-up, maybe two, would fit in it. We pretend to take a trip to Hollywood to see Ricky Nelson. Running out of gas, we decide to carry the long hose from the pump and put water into the tank.

Drifting from one thing to another, we go into the house. While Kathy looks for phone numbers under the name Nelson, I dial. In a soft voice I ask, "May I speak to Ricky, please?"

Her half hour has disappeared and it is time for her to go home. I ask, "Mom, can I go to Kathy's house to play?"

"*May* I go to Kathy's house, is the correct way to ask, and you just played."

"I know, Mom, but it wasn't enough time."

"You may go for half an hour."

The half hours always pass so quickly. Kathy asks permission to walk me home, then I get permission to walk Kathy home, and this is how it goes until Irene, my mom, or Rosemary put a stop to it. In the end, we walk halfway and return home alone.

A few days later we are sitting around the supper table and Dad mentions that little foreign car. "I turn the ignition key on, but nothing I do ignites the engine. It is a mystery because just a few days ago it was running just fine."

Mom shrugs, but I can tell she is thinking. "I can't remember exactly—" She pauses to think some more. "I know there is something." Her eyes crinkle at the brows as she looks around, then at me. "Gloria and Kathy were playing in it the other day."

Dad also turns and looks at me. I don't know what they expect of me. "We just played in it. We never turned it on; we didn't even have the keys."

"What did you play?" my father asks. His voice is not accusing.

"We took turns at the wheel pretending to drive. And we put in some gas. And then—"

Dad cut into my sentence. "You put in gas?"

I was going to say we came inside to make calls on the phone but thought better of it. Dad's voice broke my thoughts. "You mean you pretended to put in gas?"

"Well, we can't reach your tank of real gas, so we pretended water was gas."

"Gloria."

"We just used the hose and put water into the tank." Dad didn't look so happy. "That's okay, isn't it?"

For Halloween Robert and Tony use the little storage shed behind Kathy's house to make a spook house. The preparations take all week. Kathy and I want to help, but Tony made it clear they didn't want our help. "You don't know shit. Go away."

Our brothers hang tarps and sheets and use old tires and all kinds of objects found around the yard. The night of Halloween, kids from all over Corrales come to the spook house. It is totally dark inside, and we walk through at a slow pace. In some areas we crawl on squishy, cold, rubbery things that feel like snakes. Water squirted in my face causes me to cover it quickly. Flashlights reveal scary masks and I scream and wish I could close my eyes. It is a great spook house. It costs every person three pennies to go in. Kathy and I are allowed in free as many times as we want. It is less scary each time.

My parents said to be home by 8:30, and everyone has stopped coming to the spook house. We are already in costume. I am a Chinese maiden dressed in a kimono that Uncle Benny brought from Korea. Kathy has painted her eyes black like a raccoon and has freckles on her face. My sisters, Kathy, and I follow Tony and Robert with our little brown bags and walk Corrales Road. Together we yell, "Trick or treat," at every house, starting at La Entrada Road, then north to Sandoval Elementary, where we turn back. Mrs. Kinien never answers her door. No treats from her. We know her because she substitute teaches at our school. She refuses to give candy. Her lights are out and everything is dark. Tony and Robert start to scribble on Mrs. Kinien's windows with a bar of soap, and the rest of us run.

We get home with plenty of candy.

A Child Is Born

Grama Ninfa came to help Mom with the new baby. I don't know when the new baby will get here. I haven't seen a baby yet. I am so happy Grama is here. Grampa brought her and stayed two days, but he had to go back to Las Aguitas to take care of the animals. He wanted to stay and wait for the baby, but it hasn't arrived yet.

I don't know who will cook for him when he is home alone. Grama says, "Don't worry, he has plenty to eat. I canned meat, pinto beans, green beans, peas, corn, and chile. All he has to do is warm something and fry up some potatoes and he has a meal. You'll see, he'll be fine."

Sometimes I compare grandmothers. They are so different and both so important to me. Grandma Patrocinia is short and chubby. I don't remember ever thinking of Grama as tall or short, skinny or fat. She has always been soft. I like to sink my face into her cool arm or into her soft warm embrace. The whole front of her is one body, not separated into different sections for breasts or belly. It is one soft landing for my face and for my arms to wrap around.

Her entire front shakes when she laughs. Grampa keeps her in a state of laughter. Tears running down her face are common too. I remember that day when I left Mora to come to Corrales, I remember Grama telling me, "*No llores tanto mija te arrugas como yo.*" She touched her wrinkles with my hand, showing me they traveled from the corners of her eyes all the way down her cheeks to her neck. She tried to scare the tears out of me by telling me I would get wrinkles like hers. I will always remember that day. I don't like to think about it too much because I start to cry and be sad all over again. I love having Grama here. I sometimes think what it could be like if we all lived together in one house. I'd like that.

Dad took Mom to the hospital. Dolores, Grama, and I are waiting for them to call home. It is getting really late and we are getting tired. Dolores asks Grama, "Where is Mom getting the baby? They are sure taking a long time to get home."

I had not thought to ask that question, but now I want to know too. Dolores and I wait while Grama sniffs and pulls a silver bobby pin out from where it hides, then pulls loose hair back into her bun and pushes the bobby pin into place. Maybe Grama doesn't know because she is thinking really hard. I can tell by the way her eyes look straight ahead and not at us.

"She will get the baby at the hospital."

Dolores has more questions. "Can she bring more than one? Will she bring a boy or a girl? Can I stay up until they get home?"

"I want to, too, Grama. Can we, please?" I ask.

"You both have school tomorrow and they might be really late coming home. I think it is time to go to bed now. Let's say our prayers and go to sleep."

Dolores and I declare at the same time, "Oh, Grama." We obey and go to bed. I guess I am tired because I can't wait any longer. It is getting to hard to keep my eyes open.

I came to school telling everybody that my mom is bringing home a baby boy today. My teacher wants to know his name, time of birth, weight, and everything. "I'll have to tell you tomorrow because I don't know any of that. All I know is that by lunchtime today, Dad will have Mom and the baby home."

The lunch bell finally rings. I run and Tiger follows me. Dolores and Tony run past me.

At home, I see Grama but keep going to Mom's room. In the crib is the new baby. Dolores and Tony are already in the room. Mom is taking the baby out of the bassinet and is talking very softly to him. "Joseph, this is your older brother, Tony, and your sisters, Dolores and Gloria." I stare at the perfect tiny baby wrapped in blue. Mom says, "Sit on the bed and I'll let you hold him." All three of us sit really still. One by one we hold little Joseph.

My lips touch his smooth skin. "He is so soft."

Mom nods and smiles.

Grama calls from the kitchen, "Come eat."

I look at Mom. "I'm not hungry."

Mom doesn't have to say anything. I already know I must obey. After we eat I don't want to go back to school. I yell back to the baby, "See you after school, Baby."

Every day some relatives come to see our new baby brother. Even Mom's cousins who live in Albuquerque have come. Dad's sisters and brothers all come. Grandma Patrocinia and Aunt Bea are here right now. Joseph sleeps and sleeps.

Grandma Patrocinia is cradling Joseph in both arms. She says, "He is so tiny and so perfect. I wish he'd wake up so I can see his eyes." Making a cross with her thumb over her index finger, she crosses the baby's little forehead. She talks directly to Joseph, "God bless you," she says to him. Grandma always blesses us that way when we say good-bye, but today she turns to us and says, "*No le quiero dar el ojo.*"

I ask her, "What do you mean about giving him the eye?"

"Well, if we stare at a baby too long, we can cast a bad spell on him and he can get very sick."

"I still don't understand. What do you mean?" I ask.

"Well, some people think it is pure superstition, but I have seen babies get very sick. It is important to bless a baby to make sure not to give him the ojo."

"Can a baby die if someone gives him the ojo?"

"Well, the thing that you have to do is take the poor child to a man named Juan or a woman named Juanita. Juan or Juanita takes holy water in their mouth and spits at the baby's face. This will get rid of the spell and the baby can get well. I have seen babies get well immediately."

"Who, Grandma?" I ask.

"I had to take your uncle Fred to my *comadre* Juanita because somebody gave him the ojo. It was at church too. He was such a beautiful baby, just like Joseph. He was so sick for days. And he was healed immediately."

"Who is comadre Juanita? Do I know her?" I am thinking she must be some kind of miracle worker like Jesus.

"She is my sister. She baptized your daddy and that makes her my comadre."

"Daddy talks about his madrina all the time. She makes the best refried beans with red chile. He makes them like hers, kind of crispy and dry. They're good."

"She is the best godmother a boy can have." Grandma Patrocinia smiles.

I think we are all so lucky to have a new baby. Thank you, God.

Stage Pride and an Unexpected Move

My class has been rehearsing for the Christmas play and our teacher says we are ready. Mom let me wear her yellow satin Cinderella dress. She wore this beautiful dress when she played Cinderella as a young girl. The dress reaches the floor and when I touch the puffy green satin sleeves, I feel like a rich lady. Mom put red lipstick on my lips and some sweet perfume on my wrists and behind my ears. She said, "Only for tonight."

Mrs. McCarthy, now my second grade teacher, just said our performance is next. It is a cold night and we are waiting outside for the door to open so we can walk on stage. I wish I had a jacket to put on.

Climbing up the steps onto the stage, I trip on my long dress and nearly fall. I make myself stop laughing the minute I see Mrs. McCarthy. We are supposed to be sophisticated and orderly walking on stage. My friend, Clair, giggled too.

I've said my lines. Maybe I said them right, but I'm not sure about it. I hurried to get it over with. My mom and the rest of the moms clapped loud. They must have liked it. The play is over, so we can sit and listen to the rest of the grades do their acts. I can't wait to eat the cookies Mom brought. I helped her bake them today after school. She said I had to wait to eat any because they were for all the people who came to the play. I showed Kathy which cookies we made and told her to eat some.

I have returned from Mora and am now in third grade. My family keeps growing, but Kathy has a small family. A brother, mother, and father. Her father, Eduardo, fought in the Second World War and developed lung problems. Eduardo is always going back to the veterans' hospital for long stays. When he is home, we have to play outside because he has to rest. He spends a lot of time in bed.

My family is large. I have three brothers and two sisters. My dad was in Germany during the Second World War. My father is a healthy man with a wide upper body and strong hairy arms and big thick fingers and rough scratchy hands. His face and arms are dark from exposure to the sun and working outdoors.

Kathy's father, in contrast, is very pale and skinny. When he tells us stories and laughs, his laugh often turns into a deep long cough that he can't control. He often finishes his tale in a raspy, shaky tone.

One day close to the end of April, Eduardo died. After Eduardo's death I developed fears. I am afraid to go into the room where he used to rest. Sometimes walking home alone, I run past their house and past the outhouse in the neighbor's yard. Learning about souls and the Holy Ghost in catechism, I imagine Eduardo's ghost is in the outhouse.

I cannot tell my best friend that I am afraid of her dad's spirit. My fears cause me grief. Things start to happen when Kathy and I are together and alone.

Being alone, just the two of us, in Eduardo's room is difficult for me. "Did you hear that?"

"What?" Kathy is unnerved, even annoyed, with me.

"I heard a door open and close. We're alone, right? No one else is home, is there?"

"I don't hear a thing. Listen, it's quiet."

Kathy gives me confidence, and I calm my pounding heart.

We are at my house, alone, which is unusual given the size of my family. We are playing jacks on the step outside the back door close to the kitchen. I play jacks with Dolores all the time, so I am quite good and am already on Around the Worlds and she is still on Barns.

"Hey," I ask, "did you hear that?" Both of us hear the faucet in the kitchen turn on and off several times. We are bewildered. Not saying a word, we quietly rise and slowly walk into the kitchen. The sink is wet but there is no water coming from the faucet. "Let's check the bathroom. I know what I heard."

"Me too. I heard running water," she said.

While in the bathroom, the sound returns. We hurry and find the kitchen faucet on. It only takes a quick glance for me to recognize her fear as my own, and we run out the kitchen door to the road and past the neighbor's house. We reach Kathy's house in record time.

Tony and Robert come walking up the road. Tony has his hands in his pocket, swinging his shoulders from side to side, doing his tough guy walk. We tell them what just happened. They listen to our wild story and laugh.

"Don't laugh—it really happened. Go back to the house with us and look around." I put my hands together like I am praying. "Please!"

Acting bothered and yet heroic, they follow us back to my house and look around.

"You're crazy. There's nothing here to find. See, the water is off. No one is here. Just go back to playing," Tony teased and looked over at Robert and shook his head.

Several such events are taking place. It is getting too weird. The weather is warmer and Kathy and I go for walks. The ditch is always nice. Ducks swim around and we make up songs or sing with the radio. Kathy brings her transistor radio so we can listen to KQEO. On a newsbreak we hear about an escapee from the penitentiary in Santa Fe. A man is walking along the other side of the drain ditch. We both suspect without a doubt that this is the man who escaped from the penitentiary.

She whispers, "He is wearing stripes; it has to be him. Don't they wear stripes in prison?"

"He looks mean. I think it's got to be him."

"We better go tell someone."

"We better get away from here. He might see us."

Running home as fast as our legs can run, we both tell Mom about the convict at the ditch.

"You've got to call the police, Mom! He'll get away if you don't hurry." Mom listens and asks questions. Then she tells us she will take care of everything. Kathy goes home and I am so exhausted from all the excitement, I go in my room to read, the convict soon forgotten.

On Mother's Day of third grade Kathy and I make our First Holy Communion. We have catechism every Sunday after the 7:00 a.m. Mass. Mom walks the mile and a half with her five children and waits after Mass while we receive instruction. Tony Mondragon, a seminarian, teaches the first communion class. He calls me "Morning Glory" because I am ready with hand up to answer questions. Several classes are taught at the same time in the church, with only a few rows of pews to separate each class. We practice how to go to confession and receive communion.

Grampa Fidel and Grama Ninfa are here to celebrate my First Holy

Communion. Grama and I are sitting in the kitchen. I am facing her and she is turned sideways, looking at the wall. She said the priests sit like that. She pretends to be the priest and I practice telling my sins. She reminds me that disobeying is a sin, and fighting, and talking in church. Sometimes Grama focuses too much on sin. "*Es pecado*," she likes to say every little while, even while I am playing, without a single thought to sin at all.

It is Saturday and we are on our way to confession. Walking into the confessional for the first time makes me nervous. I pull the curtain back just a little bit to let light in. I am still not comfortable in the dark. It is dusty and the kneeler creaks. A figure of Father Baca's head shows through the thin cloth. To not be overheard, I whisper, "I disobeyed my mother, I talked in church, and I fought with my brothers and sisters." Just like I rehearsed with Grama. I could not think of any other sins. I leave the confessional feeling happy and relieved to be rid of my terrible sins.

Sunday morning the sky is blue, the air crisp. The first communion class lines up in front of the church to walk in, in an orderly fashion, boys all in one line and the girls in another. I lead the girls because I am the shortest and we line up shortest to tallest. I have to remember to walk slowly and go all the way to the front pews. And when it is time for communion, I lead the girls to the rail.

Father Baca puts the Host in my mouth, and being so happy to receive Jesus, I turn to smile at Mom. She doesn't smile back. Her disapproving scowl and quick finger motions tell me to turn my face back to the altar. My face heats up and I am sure everybody can see how red it is.

When Mass is over, Dickey Gutierrez and I lead the children out of church. Outside I see Aunt Beatrice and can't wait another minute, I throw my arms up to the sky and announce, "I just received the Holy Ghost!"

All the girls look equally beautiful in our white dresses, veils, and gloves. My rosary hangs between my folded hands. Parents take our pictures in front of the church. Kathy and I take some together, standing in front of the church and in front of the big cottonwood tree.

Kathy and I play every day at school and after school. Third grade is almost over. I will be going to Las Aguitas, but I will miss playing with Kathy.

Kathy's mom, Rosemary, makes us sit down on the couch. "I have something important to tell you." She is sipping a glass of water. Kathy is sitting very still, so I copy. Rosemary finishes her water and slowly walks to the kitchen to put the glass in the sink. When she walks in, I notice that there are a few tears crawling down her face. Wiping at them, she finally starts to talk. "Gloria, you are Kathy's favorite friend."

I nod. "Kathy is my favorite friend."

Rosemary smiles. "I'm glad. Listen, there is something you should know."

I look at Kathy, asking without words, *what?*

Her mother continues, "Kathy, Robert, and I will be moving to Albuquerque. We will not be neighbors anymore. Kathy will have to go to a new school."

"Not Sandoval Elementary School?"

"She will not return to Sandoval for fourth grade. I'm sorry, Gloria, but we have to move away."

Kathy and I hug and cry. "My mom made me keep it a secret. She wanted to tell you when we were all together. We are moving to Albuquerque to be close to my aunt."

Later Tony confesses, "I am going to miss Robert too." Tony must be feeling truthful because he just told me that he and Robert were the ones turning the water on and off and opening and closing doors and drawers in order to scare Kathy and me.

"Nuh-uh! You couldn't have. We looked! There was never anyone around. And besides, you helped us."

"We had to make it look like we were helping, but we hid in the closet or another room, watching the two of you scared out of your wits. It was hard to keep from laughing out loud."

Tony takes the punch to his arm. We both laugh. Remembering Kathy, I smile to myself thinking, *She will always be my special friend.*

Perra, Daddy's Home

Grama and Grampa are visiting for a few days. I didn't know they were coming. I am so happy. When I saw their yellow car drive up in our driveway, I jumped up and down and hurried to them. Grama's belly is exactly what I've needed to hug. My first words are, "How long will you be staying?"

Grama pulls me from her. "I just got here and you want me to leave already?"

"No, Grama! I just want to know how long you are staying. I wish you could live here." Sometimes I don't understand Grama. She should know that I never want her to leave.

Grama still likes her naps. I keep checking to see if she wakes up, but she continues to snore. I came in from playing jacks with Dolores, then I left Diana climbing the tree singing, "Supercalifragilisticexpialidocious" and "A Spoon Full of Sugar." On my last check I decided to sit in this chair next to where Grama naps. I'm reading *Poor Little Rich Girl*, a book about a young girl surviving in the streets of France. I can't believe all she has to go through, having no money or food. Mom passes by and whispers, "Leave her be. What is so important you can't wait till she wakes up?"

"Nothing. I just want to talk with her. She's only staying a few days, and she sleeps every day."

Grama must have heard us whispering. "Gloria, come here, mi hija, talk to me." She frowns at Mom.

Mom climbs onto the bed with us. "Oh no, you can't get rid of me that easily."

Diana and Dolores come in out of the sun and join us too. We are all squeezed in with legs hanging off the bed and arms reaching up to the ceiling and laughing.

We hear Dad's little red truck clang-clanging down the dirt road. Grama sits up. "*¡Hay perras!* You dogs, your daddy is home. *¿Qué hora es?*"

Dolores, Diana, and Mom race off to greet him.

I feel like someone should answer her, so I stay behind. "I don't know what time it is. I've got to go, Grama. Diana will beat me to Dad's lunch pail."

"What do you expect to find in there?"

"Leftover beans, or something in his thermos."

"Your poor daddy works hard all day. I don't think he'll have any leftover lunch. Besides, you just ate beans for lunch."

"He always saves us a little bit. Grama, Diana's gonna reach him first." I run out the back way, letting the screen door slam. We have always run out to greet him. Dad is climbing out of his truck and is surrounded by all his children saying all at once, "Daddy's home, Daddy's home! Hi, Daddy."

He is holding his metal lunch pail up over his head, laughing. "What more could a man want? It sure is good to get home and be greeted by my family." He hands his pail over to Diana. I peek in to see what treat he saved for us. Inside the thermos there is only about a teaspoon of beans, but he saved a little bit of pie. Diana is happy.

I am happy because Grama is visiting. She calls for us girls to go help make supper.

"I'll make the tortillas," I say.

"You can make tortillas?" she asks.

"Yep, ask my mama. I learned this year and I'm getting better every time I make them."

Some of my tortillas are crispy and some look like maps of the different states, but the others are *más o menos* round.

Grama adds butter to one of the more or less round tortillas. "*Buen hecho*, Gloria! These are very good." That's all I wanted to hear.

I think Mom is distracted by Grama's visit. Ruth, Dolores's best friend, came over a while ago and showed her a little booklet. Ruth asked if she and Dolores could show me the book, and Mom said yes.

We're walking to the far end of Ahern's field. The wind is blowing and Ruth has a scarf on her head. I wish I had worn a scarf; my ears are cold. I hope I will not get one of those fierce earaches I often get.

I don't usually get to hang out with my sister and her friend. We have stopped right under the Russian olive trees. One of the tree trunks is growing crooked and bends like it is bowing to the queen. I love the smell of the blossoms, extra sweet like the perfume Rosemary wore. For an instant I wish Kathy could be here.

Ruth opens the booklet and Dolores tells me to sit next to her and look at the book. I see black and white pictures of what they call the woman's parts. Ruth's blue eyes sparkle with excitement as she reads. They take turns reading. Dolores asks me, "Do you understand?"

I look up to the sky and admit, "No, not really."

They try to explain about how an egg travels through a tube, and then we get a period, and that means we bleed every twenty-eight days. "Now do you understand?"

I nod because really all this talk and reading is taking too long and not as exciting as I first thought it would be. I was sure fifth graders were privileged to have this booklet, but I can't see what is so great about it.

One afternoon when my parents came to pick me up from my summer stay at Grama's, my mother followed me through the plum orchard all the way back to the outhouse. She said, "I want to talk to you about something."

Curious and surprised, I said, "Sure, what?"

She asked, "Have you gotten cramps yet?"

I said, "No, but I haven't eaten anything that would give me a stomachache."

Mom laughed. Not in a condescending way, but that kind of laugh when adults think we kids say something cute. "No," she said, "your period. Have you had a monthly yet?"

I remembered the word period and I remembered the monthly bleeding from what Dolores and Ruth had read. "No, not yet."

Mom said, "Be sure and tell me when you do start, because I can help you and show you what to do."

That is what she did years later when luckily I started menstruating while I was in Corrales. She then told me that no one had explained any of this to her. She said, "When I saw blood, I thought I was dying. I was afraid to tell my mother because I thought I had done something wrong to cause it, or I had cancer or something."

"Oh God, Mom."

"Then," she said, "it stopped and I forgot about it. A month later I started bleeding again. I couldn't think of what to do. I bled on the sheets and Mom guessed. She showed me what to do." It wasn't until this discovery that my mother received any instruction. And it wasn't until much later that she learned about sex.

La Cortinita

R ita and Juan are in Corrales for a visit. I haven't seen Rita since her wedding in Mora. She left to Texas to finish her mission work and to live by Juan's family. She looks so pretty. Her hair is red instead of brown and cut very short. She looks so happy.

They drove all day. They brought a boy named Raul. He speaks only Spanish, but that is just fine because even though I have to speak English at school, I always speak Spanish at home. Rita says they will sleep over and visit for a while before driving to Mora tomorrow. I am so excited to see her.

Mom cooks steaks and potatoes for lunch. She and Rita are talking while us kids play with Raul. Raul has a nice smile with deep dimples. He is thin and taller than Tony, even though he is only seven years old. Rita teaches English, reading, math, and geography at an orphanage in Hereford, a little town in Texas, close to Mexico. Raul lives in the orphanage. I went to visit once when Aunt Mary and Uncle Manny took me with them to see Rita. That was before she was married. I played with little girls and boys in a courtyard surrounded by adobe walls. The kids were all barefoot, and we sang and danced, playing circle games. I was about five then. I don't remember Raul from that group of kids.

We have been given permission to go swimming. Tony is showing Raul all his fancy jumps from the *compuerta* to the deep water hole. Dad put in four boards to dam up the water in the acequia to irrigate. He started watering the chile fields early this morning and will irrigate the corn, and then tonight in the dark he will flood the alfalfa fields and the orchard. My sister, Diana, is jumping too. I am afraid to jump, not sure if I can swim out of the deep end to safety.

The sluice is constructed with a small flatbedlike structure before the deep hole. I want to show Raul the little space between the boards where the water flows over like a waterfall into the swim hole. I learned about the breathing space from Sally and her brother Ernie when we went swimming by their house the other day. I like to sit here and let the water flow around me. With all the noise and splashing, I have no chance to talk to Raul, so I show Tony and he brings Raul with him.

All three of us fit. The brown muddy water flows above us. We can sit under here as long as we want because we can breathe under this waterfall. Water rushes over us and splashes a little into our air pocket, but not too much. Tony breaks the flow with his hand and we get a mouthful of water. I can see through the water; it is like looking through a curtain, a *cortinita*. Images are blurry. Blinding sunrays shine through. It is too loud to carry on a conversation, but we are all smiling, trying to hear what the other is saying. I don't feel like such a chicken now because I was afraid to jump into the water.

Climbing out is tricky. I hold on to the boards that dam up the water and pull myself up out of the water. Tony and Raul have already climbed the thin wall of boards and are on the walking bridge. I am pulling myself up but the water pressure is strong. I keep trying, wishing someone would help me. Ah, finally I am able to pull up. My leg straddles the wall of boards. I attempt to stand and reach for the bridge, but I slip and fall back in the water. I am in the deep hole. I can't see anything. Oh, I remind myself, open your eyes. I want to swim up, but I panic when I remember I don't know how. My feet don't reach the bottom and I am scared to death. Raul is pulling me out of the water. I didn't see him coming and don't know when he grabbed me, but I am glad he jumped in for me. He slides on the slimy board and nearly loses control. We could slide right off again. He places me over the wall where I fell from in the first place, and Tony reaches for me. Slowly and carefully, he pulls and Raul pushes. I am on the walking bridge and safe. I cry and feel embarrassed. I want to go home.

At home we tell how Raul saved my life. He is my hero. I act like I was not afraid, but I know how scared I was of drowning. Of course we get the lecture about being careful in the ditch from Mom. Then Dad says, "I should have been with you guys. I should've never let you go without a grown-up."

Qué Bueno Que Se Acabo la Escuela

S chool is out for the summer, each summer's gift. Mora changes little from year to year. Coming back to Grama and Grampa's farm is my pot of gold at the end of the rainbow. Grampa is the same ol' kidder. He tells riddles and stories just like always. He uses a play-on-words to be funny. We play checkers and cards every night while Grama makes dinner. Grama continues to read to me and I read to her, only now in English. Her constants are prayer, song, whistles, and sniffles, soft warm eyes, cushy embraces, and shy smiles. They are all I needed for a welcome home reception.

This time when I return to my grandparents' home, I am not the queen bee anymore. Lucille, my cousin, has come to stay the summer too. She takes away some of their attention. I have to share them with her. It is not exactly the way I like it to be, but it turns out I get used to it pretty quickly. I now have a constant companion. I no longer have to carry a two-way conversation with myself. She keeps me out of trouble, and because I don't enjoy visits to Aunt Mary's house, I'm glad Lucille goes in my place. Eloy is gone to the army. Viola has gone to Corrales to help my parents with childcare while Mom is at work.

I turn a dark shade of green when I discover I am going back to Corrales, but Lucille is not going back to Santa Fe. She is getting to stay with Grama and go to school in Mora. How can that be? What about me? My position is being filled by an imposter, a not so deserving granddaughter—can't have that. I thought I was the most special.

While I was in Mora I paid more attention to Grampa's riddles. I memorized a few and am anxious to challenge siblings and friends in Corrales. Eager to show off, I make my brother my first target. "Hey, Tony, I bet you can't figure out this *adivinanza*." I myself had to be shown how the riddle works, but I am not telling him that.

"*Viente patos y viente patas metí dos en un cajón. ¿Cuántas patas y picos son?*"

He struggles for a little bit before saying, "Oh, you and your stupid riddles."

Maybe my approach upset him. I could have simply asked him to figure it out, but the fact that he doesn't give much effort hurts my feelings. "They are not stupid. Grampa taught me them." I know he thinks the world of Grampa too, and I am sure he will reconsider his opinion once he realizes it came from Grampa, but he just walks away with a backward wave of the hand.

Dolores, like just about everybody else I ask, does her best. She thinks out loud: "Twenty male ducks plus twenty female ducks equal forty ducks. Forty ducks will have forty beaks and eighty feet. The answer is one hundred and twenty. Yes! That's it: one hundred twenty."

I love this part as much as my grandfather does. "No! Not right. Try again." No matter how much she tries, the answer keeps coming out wrong.

Because Dolores is my older sister and I think everything about her is the MOST, I take her aside and teach her what my grandfather has taught me. "Okay, Dolo, think about what I'm saying. I'll say it very slowly this time so you can catch on. *Veinte patas y veinte patos metí dos en un cajón. ¿Cuántas patas y picos son?*"

She reacted pretty much the same as me.

"Oh! Now I get it! You put two in a box. That makes two beaks and four feet making the answer SIX. Right?"

La Vecina

School is not the same without Kathy. Louise is my new friend. She came to live with her aunt, La Vecina, our neighbor. Louise, her older sister, and her mother are our neighbors now too. It is hard to say where they all sleep. La Vecina has seven children still living at home. Gina is my friend, Ray is Tony's friend, and Suzi is Dolores's friend. Her husband, don Juan, is a sheepherder in Utah and only comes home occasionally.

La Vecina takes great care to keep her family safe when he is away. Whenever a stranger comes onto her property, we hear a gunshot in the air as a warning. "*¿Quién eres y qué haces aquí?*" I am glad she asks for their identity and their reason for being there before shooting them. We know she will undoubtedly use that rifle if necessary. Strangers better believe it too.

Our three friends come to our house to play and sometimes Louise is with them. We spend a lot of time at their house too. When it's time to come home, Mom uses her loudest call to summon us. Our houses are separated by three acres of fields, an orchard, a drain ditch, and a small utility road. No big deal for Mom—she has what it takes to call us home. "Come and get it," means it's time to eat. We can hear her but don't always obey. Mom can get louder if she has to.

La Vecina tells me some interesting stories about the past when she lived in Chamita. She talks about things that no one in my family talks about. She once said, "There is a river running underground right under my house. I can hear it at night when everybody is asleep and the house is very quiet. If you get really quiet right now, you will be able to hear it." I tried, but I only heard regular noises like birds tweeting and dogs barking. My father says La Vecina helps people find water in their property when they are getting ready to dig a well. He said they call people like her a "water witch."

The stories we hear at La Vecina's house scare me half to death. *La bruja* or *el brujo*, I am told, will change into a coyote or an owl. Brujos can be good or bad witches, psychics, or maybe people with medicinal powers.

El Diablo, the Devil, might appear as a handsome man with dark black wavy hair and light creamy skin. I could be in the outhouse and see the head of a goat with long whiskers and bulging eyes hanging in the corner. It could definitely, according to my friend, be el Diablo. I must be alert at all times to my surroundings because I'll never know when or where these apparitions might appear.

On winter nights, sitting close to the wood-burning stove in a lowly lit room, we listen to long spooky stories from La Vecina. When the hour to walk home arrives, we run. My short legs spin with fright. Everyone is faster than me and I cry, "Wait for me." Tony usually backtracks to reprimand or be supportive. I never know which and I don't care as long as he comes for me. Sometimes Dolores takes pity on me.

Louise's mother has large cheekbones that stick out of her skeleton-shaped face. Her clothes hang loosely on her bony arms and legs. Dark eyes are shadowed in dark circles and look vacant in their sockets. I truly believe she is the bruja in all the stories they tell. Why is it that none of them are afraid of her? They love their aunt. In fact, they seem to love her more than their own mother.

I hang back and hope she does not notice me. If she speaks directly to me, I answer quickly. A row of straight corn-shaped teeth in a lipless mouth is of no comfort to me. That grin teases as though she has secret knowledge about me. I want to go play and get away from her, right now. In fact, I want *her* to go back to where she came from. She is nothing like La Vecina.

Louise, her sister, and her mother will be moving to Albuquerque soon. As I became familiar with Louise's mother, I lost the fear I once experienced. I began to see that she was a normal, kind woman like her sister, and not a bruja. Perhaps there are no real brujas. And if there are, I don't know any. I'm going to miss Louise.

Dad is building a garage behind the house. He is using block instead of adobe. La Vecina's sons, Isidoro and Emilio, come to help Dad sometimes. Their mother sends them to help. Dad has been told not to pay them. La Vecina says, "That is what neighbors are for. I have to teach my boys how to help others." But Dad reaches into his wallet and sneaks a few bills to them now and then.

Our other neighbor, Felipe, helps Dad with the garage too. He once helped Dad wire our house. He had spools of telephone wire that he used to string electricity from his house to ours while Dad built. Dad used that telephone wire for electricity in our bedroom and in his and Mom's room. For Christmas last year Mom hung a wreath on a wire that stuck out of the outside wall where one day Dad will put an outdoor light. The house started smelling like something was burning. We all went around sniffing and trying to locate where the smell was coming from. Mom quickly turned off the breaker, and the wires were the only things that had burned. Dad had to rewire the two bedrooms.

Sometimes during harvestime, La Vecina sends her sons to help pick chile. She does not want Dad to pay them for that either, so he sends them home with sacks of chile.

Our chile fields are full of people at harvest time. My aunts, uncles, friends, and even Grandma Patrocinia and Grandpa Jesús come to help us pick sacks and sacks of chile. The chile is kept in the walk-in cooler until sold. If we deliver sacks to customers, we wet the gunnysack to keep it cool and keep the chile crisp. Dad tries to keep all customers pleased and satisfied by selling only the best chile.

When we have too much chile in the walk-in cooler, we fill the truck and drive to Albuquerque. We go from door to door in a neighborhood by Pat Hurley Park to sell chile in buckets for fifty cents. If they want more, we sell them a sack or two. Dad instructs us to let people break a chile to taste it if they want to test the heat. We say it's hot if they want hot and not so hot if they don't want hot. Dad wants us to say, "Come to our house in Corrales if you need more chile. There will be plenty of red later on." If they ask for directions, we give them our phone number and say, "There is also a sign at the road."

La Vecina is always helping. Mom tells us that when she and Dad first moved to Corrales, La Vecina heard Mark crying. They were out in the fields working and Mark was just a baby. La Vecina came and took Mark to her house so that my parents could keep working. Later, she took care of Mark for eight months when Mom went back to work in the city. She would not take pay. "That's what neighbors are for," she often says.

Tiendita de San Juan

Daddy drove us to the north end of Corrales and into the bosque to dump a load of trash. Other people are also here getting rid of trash. The piles of garbage are enormous, like little mountains. We run around as though it is a treasure park and hunt for goodies. Dad tells Tony, Dolores, Diana, and me that we can take one item home. Our neighbors are here too, and Rupert tells his children that this is *"la tiendita de San Juan,"* the little shop of Saint John. I found a play cash register and ask if I can take it home. Mom lets me.

Daddy whistles for all of us and says, "It's time to go." We climb into the back of the truck, happy with our new toys. He drives farther into the bosque and stops right next to the river. Everybody jumps out of the truck. Dad yells, "Wait, I need to check how deep the water is." With a long branch in hand, he reaches as far into the water as he can and sticks it into the river. "It is too deep here. The water is moving too fast."

We move to a place that he thinks is safer and are allowed to get into the river. He has stressed over and over that we are not ever allowed to swim in the river if he is not with us. I am afraid we have not always obeyed that order either.

After our swim we dry off with towels Mom brought for us. Lying on our backs, we choose cloud shapes to fit our imaginations. Mom reads a book and Dad takes a little walk.

When he returns, he has us all get in a huddle. "I saw some wildlife. Walk with me and I'll show you, but you have to be very quiet." Holding a finger to his lips, Dad leads the way, lifting his feet and letting them drop softly. We imitate his walk and follow without making a sound.

We watch a heron's pencil shape drift across the river. Mallard ducks dunk heads to find food. A hawk with a red tail glides in circles until he disappears.

Madre Mía

Every night before going to sleep after I say my prayers, I always say, "Kiss to Jesus and kiss to the Madre Mía." I kiss my fingers and throw a kiss to the air. I don't remember who taught me to send kisses to Mother Mary and Jesus, but now it is a habit.

Today during Mass Tony and I got in trouble. Mom scolded, "When we get home, you will be punished." Our walk home takes at least half an hour. I cannot think what made her mad this time. I wish I could skip and run and laugh like the others, but I know what's coming. Tony doesn't seem concerned at all.

After our spanking, Mom sends us to her bedroom. I am told to get on my knees and pray nine rosaries. Tony has to pray three. While Tony is in the room with me, it doesn't feel like a horrible punishment because he makes me laugh. He mimics Mom and makes angry faces and pretends to spank me. Our giggles bring Mom to the room. "Silence. Pray in silence. If it takes you all day to say your rosaries, it takes you all day, but you have to stay on your knees until you're done."

Once Tony finishes his rosaries, I beg Mom to let me go too, but she says no. I hear conversation coming from the kitchen and smell roast beef. Then I hear laughter and feet running outside the window. This punishment is harder than any I can remember. Mom's spankings are usually over and done with in a matter of minutes. I can close my ears to her screaming and yelling—those reprimands are over quickly too. This feels like I am a very bad girl and only Jesus can help such a bad girl. It feels as long as the silent treatments I get when Mom has implemented the silence that can last days.

I am not certain if I finished my rosaries. When I wake up, I find solace in a beautiful dream:

The Blessed Virgin Mary is tall. I can tell she is not a statue. She stands under an arch of large blue Christmas lights. She and the room glow in the soft blue light. Mother Mary, whom I call Madre Mía, gazes at me. Her head is slightly bent to one side and her eyes look straight into mine. She slowly pulls her praying hands apart and reaches for me in a gentle gesture full of kindness. I want to reach for her hand and go away with her, but I hold back. She bows her head, nods, and closes her eyes, then reopens them and looks directly at me. I am uncertain if she says the words or if I just understand her meaning: "It's alright." My eyes are fixed on her. Her words are now clear, "*Te amo, Gloria.*"

This is how the dream ends. I think her words will help me any time I feel unloved and troubled. The dream also made me realize I miss Grama so much.

Tadpoles and Papalotes

Sometimes I have so much fun with my brothers and sisters. Other times I would like to run away and go back to live with Grama and Grampa in Mora. It's not only that they don't want to play with me, it is that they actually fight with me. Diana and Dolores have even said they hate me. Hate is such a mean word. I can't think of anyone I hate. I think if a person hates someone it means that they wish they were dead. If I cry, they call me Cry Baby.

It sure doesn't help to tell Mom about it. She can't stand it when we fight. She has spanked me when I cry and says, "You want something to cry about? I'll give you something to cry about." Then I cry even more. She says, "That's enough. Stop that crying or you'll get some more."

Spankings come for no apparent reason sometimes. Tony helps Mom catch us if we run away. The jarita, the small branch of a willow tree, sure does hurt. I have tried yelling, "Sorry, I'm sorry!" Those words usually stop Mom when she is spanking Dolores, but they don't work for me.

There are times I answer back. Mom will smack me across the face. I react to her yelling and she reacts to my smart mouth. It's crazy.

I pretend that I will leave and go live with Grama and Grampa. I know deep inside that I will not be allowed to, but I imagine it anyway. When I feel alone, I walk to the bosque, dragging my stick behind me. I lie on the board that crosses the drain ditch and look at the blue sky and listen to the water flow and gurgle. I stay as long as it takes for me to feel better, then I walk home.

Name-calling is one way to get each other to cry or fight. Daddy calls us animals when we fight. He says, "Humans are basically animals. There is a real fine line between human and animal."

I don't like for him to call us animals. I value his opinion of me and feel badly that he thinks of us like that. I have cried and he has apologized, but then he does it again. If he meant his apology, he would not do it again. He even said, "I'm sorry, hija. I don't know what makes me say those things."

Roly-poly, Fatso, Tadpole, and Scaredy-cat are names Tony calls me. Tadpole embarrassed me because he called me that in front of our friends. We were all playing at the drain ditch. The boys were catching frogs, minnows, and tadpoles. I refused to touch their slimy trophies. My goal was not to catch any, but to find which tadpoles had metamorphosed. "That one has sprung legs. I see one without a tail."

Tony turned to me and said, "You look like a tadpole. All round on top and skinny legs." I laughed only to hide my real feelings.

I never laugh when Tino Leal calls me Bucky Beaver. Oh, he is cruel. He tells other kids, "You can tell she was out last night. Just look at all the trees she knocks down and chews up with her teeth." He should talk; his teeth stick out more than mine.

My sisters and I sing, "Tony Baloney went to town riding on a pony. Stuck a feather in his cap and called it macaroni." He doesn't like it. On the way to school there are two brothers we can't stand. They are mean to Tony and Dolores. They throw rocks at my brother and sister. At school they call my brother Blackie Carbon. His skin is a little browner than mine. I could just kick those two bullies.

Older boys call Mark Papalote and Mad Magazine. Mark is such a handsome boy; I don't know why they tease like that. I don't even understand what they mean. All I know is that when we call each other names at home, it is almost okay, but when other people outside the family name-call, I get angry and feel bad.

Daddy Long Legs is what Dad started calling Diana. She is younger than me and keeps passing me in height. When Dad teases, he is gentle with Diana. Me, I get mean because she is mean with me. We fight, pulling hair and scratching. I get my hands in her hair and she scratches. We call, "Give?" but neither of us give in. She is so strong that I want to cry, but I pretend she isn't hurting me at all.

Diana's wild curly mass of hair has also earned her the name Geronimo. She cries when we call her that. She cries more about that than when we hurt each other physically. Sometimes I feel bad for teasing her. Then I remember how mean she is to me.

Dolores wants to tame Diana's hair and comb it for her, but Diana will not let her get close with a brush or comb. This is when Dolores says, "You want it wild, go ahead."

Dolores is a toothpick. She fits the name Toothpick. I only call her that when she calls me Fatso. Dolores is tall and skinny. I think her legs are as thin as my arms. I don't think I am fat, but everybody in my family thinks so. My face is round and my tummy sticks out. I think they are all too thin.

Aunt Viola taught me a little rhyme that I can tell people when they tease me. Sticks and stones can break my bones, but words will never hurt me. I use the verse, but it doesn't seem to stop Tony or that ugly Tino. Oh well.

Qué Bueno Que Se Acabo la Escuela

Grampa sings this to me every summer when I return to Mora. To my surprise, I discover that in two weeks Lucille will return to Santa Fe for the summer. All is well. I think Grama would be upset if she knew I am jealous, but I can't help it. I am also happy that Viola is going to Corrales for the summer to help again. Mom has six children and has returned to work.

Now that I am older, I walk the mountain and go on picnics by myself as far as the spring with the clay. I make clay pots, dolls, and figurines. I read books, pretend as much as always, and make friends with the forest. I talk with the trees and listen to the wind and watch the clouds form shapes just for me.

When we shop for groceries, Grama spends extra money and buys a large jar of dill pickles, all for me. She lets me help with laundry, mattress cleaning, summer painting, and window repair. A windowpane broke and needs to be replaced, but we are not making a trip to Las Vegas for a while.

I am totally impressed that Grama is planning to fix the window without glass. "How?" I ask. She is used to my questions and hears the doubt in my voice.

"Bring me a *jumate* full of flour."

I hurry and fill a small pan with flour and bring it to her. "I can't see how flour will fix your window."

"Now bring me water *en la olla de diez*."

I carry a small bucket of water and place it by her side. Grama mixes flour with water to make a paste. She unfolds newspaper and glues it to where the pane is missing. "You add paste and another sheet of newspaper and keep doing that until you have at least six layers. After it dries it will keep the wind, rain, and cold out."

Our temporary window lasts until we make a trip to Vegas, and could make it through the winter, if you ask me.

Grama likes showing me how to do things and I like learning from her.

One of Grampa's old stories about Grama is the one about her being asked to be a teacher: "When your grama graduated from eighth grade, the nuns wanted her to teach. She didn't want to. I don't see why—she is my favorite teacher, and the best teacher I ever had. She taught me to read and write.

"You see, I only went up to third grade. I was in third grade for three years. *Era muy burro yo,* way too stubborn to learn. Finally my third grade teacher said, '*Ya estás barbón,* with that beard, maybe you are too old for third grade.'"

"Your teacher was mean," I said.

Grampa jokes about things and sometimes I realize he is joking only when he laughs. "My teacher never did say such things, but I felt old. Every year I had to leave school to help my father on the farm. I started school later than the other kids because of the harvest and left earlier in the spring because it was time to plant. I wasn't catching up and it was foolish to try, so I quit going."

Grampa had to give up school for farming. I love school. Going into fifth grade is a bit scary because I will be going to a new school, but not being able to attend school at all would be very sad.

OLOS

Our Lady of Sorrows School is a parochial school in Bernalillo, and Father Baca is the pastor. He gives Mass in Corrales at our mission church. He has been preaching at San Ysidro about the Catholic school in Bernalillo for two years. He is offering to bus children from Corrales to Bernalillo if he finds enough interest.

The bus picks Dolores, Diana, and me up in front of Sandia Bar on Ella Drive at seven o'clock in the morning. It comes from the north end of Corrales and proceeds across the Rio Grande Bridge to Alameda for more students.

Father Baca drives north and makes one stop at Sandia Pueblo, where at least fifteen kids get on. We are all crowded now, and there is only standing room on the bus, so most of the Pueblo students stand. The school is five miles from here.

In my bus high school girls have hair piled high in beehives and carry huge purses. High school boys have greased down hair, looking like Elvis Presley. And there are kids all the way down to first grade, wearing braids and ponytails.

Our Lady of Sorrows School goes from first grade to twelfth. Dolores is in the seventh grade, I am in the fifth, and Diana is in the third. My brothers go to Sandoval Elementary School. Tuition for a parochial school is costly for my parents. In fact, they have made arrangements for us to clean the bus as part of our tuition. I don't mind because climbing on top of the bus is fun for Diana and me. Dolores hides when her friends pass by. She is embarrassed about cleaning the bus.

Miss Madrid is my teacher. She is young, right out of school, and is the answer to the desperate last-minute prayers for a fifth-grade teacher. Sometimes she speaks to us in half Spanish and half English. This is so different from Sandoval Elementary, where I got my hair pulled and head banged on the desk if I spoke any Spanish. Miss Madrid is about five foot three, a little round in the face and belly, wears black horn-rimmed glasses, and her hair is brown, hanging over her shoulders in soft curls. Her side tooth sits in front of the front tooth and sticks out a little when she pulls her lips back in a large smile.

Our classroom is a barrack placed behind the building where the sixth-, seventh-, and eighth-grade classes are held. A large cottonwood tree keeps us from burning up and is a perfect place to eat our lunch. Sister Sylvan, the eighth-grade teacher, is the principal of the school.

Everybody in my fifth-grade class is a stranger to me, but at recess a really nice girl named Charlotte invites me to join her group of friends. Her friends are Camilla, Geraldine, and Yolanda. Charlotte asks another new girl to play with us too. Her name is Sally. We slide down a long metal slide and chase each other and run around the dirt playground. It is almost the same here at Our Lady of Sorrows as at my old school.

At the end of the day I see my sisters in the bus. Diana is sitting with a girl from Sandia Pueblo and Dolores is sitting with a girl she met last year when she came to this school. I see Sally and sit with her. We make plans to sit together in the morning.

Father Baca, bus driver, pastor, and religious instructor, is a young priest. He is serious about his charges as parish priest. Snow or sunshine, school will go on. One time snow fell all night and piled thirteen inches deep. Father did not chance moving the school bus, but instead came for us in a car. He was by himself. Dolores, Diana, and I waited at the bus stop and Father Baca obliged us. Going north on Corrales Road instead of our regular Alameda route, Father stopped for a few other kids and packed us in like sardines. Some parents kept kids home, and other kids were told by Father to go back home for the day. He drove us to Bernalillo on a back road, a single-lane dirt path cut out by people making a shortcut from Bernalillo to Corrales. Dust usually blows so hard it is difficult to see cars and trucks as they climb into view before dropping from view in these hills. Only an experienced driver like Father Baca could find his way through the snow-burdened desert path. We arrived at school to find many students wrapped in coats and hats playing in the parking lot.

Mom met Mrs. Moreno at a church function. Mrs. Moreno and Mrs. Burlbaw are forming a women's group called the Catholic Daughters of the

Americas, the counterpart of the Knights of Columbus, the men who serve the church.

My dad converted the two-car garage behind our house into two rooms. One room is for butchering equipment, a walk-in freezer, a meat grinder, saws, and a counter for wrapping, all made out of stainless steel. The second room is for a freezer to keep all the meat in. Mom put a couch, a table, and some chairs in there. The Catholic Daughters meet in this room once a month.

It all seems so secretive. Only members can attend, and you have to be eighteen to be a member. We can help set up chairs and carry refreshments to the room and greet the women, but when the meeting starts, we must leave.

Anna Marie is Mrs. Moreno's oldest daughter and exactly my age, ten. I hadn't ever noticed them at school or church. Anna Marie's mother wanted a nice friend for her daughter and brought her to our house to play with me while the women have the meeting.

Anna Marie is tall and thin with pretty black hair that reaches the bottom of her back. She looks exotic, like the picture of Hawaiian girls on an album cover we own. Anna Marie walks slowly and never gets dirty. She sits like a lady and doesn't want to play. My other sisters left us alone after their curiosity wore off.

Then suddenly one day Anna Marie is the new student in my classroom. Father Baca stops for Anna Marie and her sister, Mimi, on Coronado Road in Corrales. My friend Sally and I sit together and sometimes invite Anna Marie to sit with us. I am getting to know her better. I see her at church and school, and sometimes her family comes to our house to visit.

It is dark and I have already had supper. Invited to spend the night, I first entered Mrs. Moreno's living room with my parents, but they have already gone home. Anna Marie has asked me to follow her. "You can put your bag in here. This is my room." It is a nice room. Everything matches: dresser, desk and chair, chest of drawers, and beds. Her mirror and shelves are all white with gold trim.

At home, I share a room with my two sisters and we have two twin beds that Uncle Manny made. The head and footboards are made of pine, carved into Southwestern floral patterns, the same pattern he uses on all his furniture from chairs to chest of drawers. Nothing else in our room matches, and it is not as tidy either.

I am not sure what to do.

"Let me put your bag over here." Anna Marie places my bag in the closet. I don't move, waiting to see what comes next.

I have spent many nights at Sally's house, and she comes to my house often too. We giggle and play and run around having fun. I play with her sisters too, Gloria and Betty. Her brother Ernest is funny and likes to tease just like my brother, Tony. Being at Sally's house is like being at home.

"Do you want to read or something?" Anna Marie asks.

"Sure, I guess so."

I look at the bookshelf, not knowing what to choose, but she gives me a book and then sits on her bed, so I sit on the other bed. A baby is crying and I hear other small voices coming from other parts of the house. Anna Marie flips a page, and even though I love to read, I can't concentrate. I am quiet because she is quiet.

Her mother opens the door and smiles. "Girls, come into the living room. I made caramel corn." I follow Anna Marie down the hallway to a room at the center of the house, where her whole family sits on a couch and some chairs. Mrs. Moreno hands over a bowl of caramel corn to be passed around. She sits at the piano and plays some very pretty music. Soon Mr. Moreno takes her place and plays, and then Anna Marie plays a couple of tunes. All the music sounds very nice.

There is a pause, and I wish they would play some more. I want to hear more. Sitting between Veronica and Mimi with my hands on my lap and listening to the keys make soft music reminds me of Grama's attic and the Victrola waltz we danced together.

Anna Marie brought her Barbie doll to school. Not one other girl in our fifth-grade class has one. We all want a chance to dress and play with Barbie during lunch recess. At the end of the day when the bell rings for dismissal, Sally, Anna Marie, and I have the pretty doll and her accessories spread out under the big tree by our classroom. Anna Marie opens the small closet with pretty little dresses, and we dress Barbie and take her to the ball and other fun places.

Every day Father Baca gives the students fifteen minutes to get on the bus before jumping in and driving off. The high school students from the building across the street usually walk over with books in hand. Viola, Sally's sister, is always holding hands with Albert, her boyfriend. Enriques walks Genova to the bus, and they talk until it is time to leave. Tillie and Emily walk with shoulders back and chins up. Older students look very important and responsible.

Time slips away in our Barbie world, and when we pack up and walk to the bus, the parking lot is empty, no bus or people in sight, nothing. I wonder if they looked for us. Did my sisters miss me? Did Sally's family notice she was not in the bus? What about Mimi, did she say anything to Father Baca about Anna Marie?

Hoping for a miracle, I look around for the bus. "Oh boy, are we in trouble!"

"How will we get home?" Sally whispers as though the quiet parking lot might hear. "My mom doesn't drive, and by the time my dad gets home, it'll be dark."

The three of us turn to the sound of the rectory door. Father Sandoval, the assistant pastor, comes out with a bundle of books and finds three little girls in a huddle, moaning about their worries. He learns that Mrs. Moreno is probably the only driver available to come for us. "Let me call your mother," he says to Anna Marie.

We wait anxiously. I have no idea if she will come for us or not. The three of us sit on the steps of the rectory and whisper. Is it because we think we will be in less trouble if we make little noise? Sally speculates, "I suppose Father Sandoval can drive us home if no one else can come for us."

Father Sandoval appears and sits with us on the steps. "Mrs. Moreno agreed to come for you. Just sit here and wait." He doesn't say anything about punishment, yet I know as well as I know anything that punishment will come. We wait and wait.

I am so happy to see Anna Marie's mother. Parking her Volkswagen without turning off the ignition is a sure sign she is in a hurry. She sends Anna Marie to thank Father and let him know we are leaving. I sit in the backseat with Sally. Mrs. Moreno turns to me and says, "I called your mother. She knows I am bringing you home."

I nod and say, "Thank you."

Sally is dropped off first. Her mother comes to thank Anna's mom for the ride. Father Sandoval had called Mrs. Sandoval to make sure she knows Sally is okay.

I pray to Jesus, "Mom is going to be mad. Just don't let her be too mad. I know I'll get a spanking; I deserve it, but please don't let her embarrass me in front of Mrs. Moreno and Anna Marie."

For punishment, I have to take Diana's turn for dishes. I was so sure that I'd get a huge spanking. Mom did say, "You make sure not to ever miss that bus again. You put a lot of people through a lot of worry and trouble over this."

Clyde, one of the boys in my class, is about four foot three, with blondish-brown hair that stands straight up in spikes like thick blades of grass. He wears faded navy-blue uniform pants that are held up by a brown belt that is too long. The extra leather hangs from the buckle, flapping about. His white shirt rarely remains tucked and blouses loosely half in, half out of his pants.

Clyde is the one who is always in trouble with the teacher. Today is our fun day. Miss Madrid brought cookies and we are having a dance contest. She brought a record player to school and we dance to Chubby Checkers's "The Twist." Joseph Ortiz and I twist our little bodies up and down and all around, earning first place. A holy card is not the prize a ten-year-old prays for, but the title of best dancer is a great honor for me. Clyde—he gets a spanking, and our day turns ugly!

"I don't want to dance," Clyde insists. Girls do not want to dance with him either. Our teacher persists and he resists. He pulls back when Miss Madrid nudges him forward. Frowning, he shakes his head strongly. "You can't make me, blankety blank blank. I hate you." Miss Madrid quickly has all the girls form a line. She has us take turns spanking Clyde with a two-by-two pine board as he leans over her desk. At first Clyde acts like a smart aleck, but the humiliation gets the best of him, and his remarks are swallowed up by his quiet shame.

Every time he gets hit I move farther back in the line. Tomasita is the tallest and strongest girl in our class. She spreads her legs, holds the board like a baseball bat, and swings. A loud "whack" ricochets off Clyde's buttocks.

Clyde cries. For some reason I cry too. I hope the bell will ring so I can leave. I plead with the teacher. Her reply is, "If one does it, all of you do it, *or* you will be punished as well." I keep praying the bell will ring, but finally it is my turn to do as I am told, but I don't like it.

Qué Bueno Que Se Acabo la Escuela

Mom has gone back to work and needs more help at home. Dad could use my help too. I am told that I will be going to Mora, but not for a few weeks.

Back in mid-April, Dad planted three acres of chile and four acres of corn next door, on land he leases from Mr. Ortiz. Our three acres of alfalfa began to turn green almost the first time Dad irrigated it. Cows and horses graze on the other six acres Dad leases from Mr. Ahern. Large hogs are fenced in the apple orchard, digging holes and making messes.

Out of school for the summer, every morning at five o'clock we get out of bed to the familiar call of Dad's voice, "Rise 'n' shine." We jump into our clothes and head for the garden.

The dawn is cool and the dirt smells like rain. Fresh air hits our faces, and hats keep the sun out of our eyes. We hurry past the pasture and over the little ditch to our garden. Dad says, "*Gracias a mi Tata Dios por otro día.*" I like that he calls God "Daddy." Grampa and Grama used to give thanks for the morning too.

With hoes in hand, we begin to cut weeds ever so carefully, so as not to injure the baby chile plants. Every now and then you hear someone say, "Oh no."

Daddy is very patient with me when I accidentally cut down a plant. "Don't worry about it. We all do that every now and then." With two fingers he takes the little green sprouts and throws them over his shoulder. "Get on your knees, like this." One knee rests on the ground while he leans over the second bent leg. "And pluck the weeds around the chile first, then sink the hoe into the ground and slide it toward the plant, making a little mound around it." His hoe has a short handle and is very sharp. I like the rhythm he makes when his hoe hits the dirt. Pum, pum, shwish, shwish; pum, pum, shwish, shwish. "Go ahead. Try it."

Tony yells out, raising his hoe in the air, "I finished my first row!" He is usually the one to finish first. Around ten o'clock, we count our rows to see who hoed the most. Tony wins most of the time, but I came in first once. Each of us can complete two or three long rows in a morning. We move slower when the plants are very tiny.

Our sweaters are retrieved and we race to the ditch. Our short swim cools off our bodies, and now we are hungry for breakfast. Midafternoon we will be allowed to go for another swim. When the sun sets, we will return to hoe until it is too dark to make out plant from weed. When the entire garden is clean, we will rest a week or more before we start all over again. Dad uses the tractor to weed the cornfield. He makes sure not to harm the tiny plants growing on the borders. When the corn plants are a few inches tall, we will hoe the cornfield too. Once they are a foot tall, we can stop hoeing. Dad claims, "The weeds will not choke out the corn because the corn grows faster than the weeds."

After dinner we are allowed to play with our neighbors. Sometimes we play hide and seek in the dark. Other times, with outside lights to light our way, we play Annie Over. A ball is thrown over the roof and caught by the team on the other side of the house. The whole team runs to the other team, but only one person has the ball hidden behind his or her back. The ball is thrown and hits someone from the opposing team. The person hit goes to his or her new team. In the end almost all the players are on one side of the house.

When my parents are ready for sleep, they call an end to our play around ten o'clock.

I finally make my departure and will arrive in Mora in three hours. Mom's cousin Julia is driving us.

Mora is getting rain every day in the middle of the afternoon. It is one of those summers when rain can turn to hail and days get so dark, they look like nights. Grama prays and performs her rain stopping rituals, but the scary storms continue. Grampa has come home out of the hard storm. In spite of the rain, I am happy to be here.

Hell, Where Is It?

Clyde did not return to our school. Tomasita, other students, and myself went on into the sixth grade as though nothing had ever happened. Clyde was not the only student to decline coming back to Our Lady of Sorrows; our class shrunk to a mere eighteen students. Last year we were twenty-seven.

I am not prepared for the likes of Sister Rosine Marie. I am not so sure she will make her way out of hell, when she dies. This nun hates me. Is it because I talk to Sally during class? Well, now she has separated us. We still send notes back and forth—what does she think we're going to do?

As time passes Sister hates me more. If God is love, is hate the devil? I am having terrible headaches that hurt so much. My vision is blurred, objects are cut in half, and flashes of light weave in colors of greens, blues, and red. When I get these headaches I feel nauseated and sometimes I vomit. I can't read very well because some of the letters are hidden in blackness so that I see only parts of words, and half of my tongue numbs.

Sister Caca, my new nickname for her, is having us read. "Gloria," she says, indicating my turn.

We are always to address her by name before we talk. "Sister Rosine Marie," I address her royal hiney, "I have a great big headache and can't read."

"You read page one hundred twenty-two from top to bottom," she demands.

My tongue is numb. I know what I am reading, but the sounds out of my mouth are not clear. I start to cry.

"Keep reading. And the word is 'the,'" she says, mocking me.

I try again and cannot see the page. "Sister," I say, "I can't read. My head really hurts."

"Oh, you poor little girl. You can't read because your head hurts."

"Sister, can I please go to the bathroom?" I beg. "I think I am going to be sick."

"No, you may not!" she snaps.

I have lost my lunch. I can't believe it. My shoes are a mess, the floor is a mess, and even my desk is splattered. I really don't care what she does to me now. I want to yell at her. She has embarrassed me in front of the whole class.

I run out of the room, tears streaming down my face. I run straight for the girl's bathroom. I never want to go back there. I rinse my mouth, then my face, hands, and shoes. Water feels so good. I can't stop crying. My head hurts so much.

I don't want to go back, but if I don't, she will only get meaner. She lives to be a witch.

I finally get enough courage to walk through my classroom door. Not one second after I enter, she commands, "Now you can clean up the mess you made."

Smelling my own vomit almost makes me throw up again. I wipe up the floor and desk. My whole body is tense and my head still hurts, but I do as I am told.

About a month later my sister Diana got sick in her fourth-grade classroom. Sister Rosine Marie demanded I go clean up my sister's vomit. I wanted to cry. Diana was sent to our cousin's house in Bernalillo to recover and was brought back after school to catch the bus home.

This nun makes fun of me when I sing. I know I am not the best singer in the world, but I love to sing. She compares me to Dolores, my older sister. "I hear your sister Dolores can sing. And she is very smart. Why aren't you like her? I hear your sister Dolores is such a good girl. Why aren't you more like her?" I have an enemy. No matter what I try to do to mend things with her, nothing works.

My mother tells me, "You have to respect your elders. She is a nun and you need to respect her. What are you doing to make her act this way?"

I give up.

This nun gives me F's on my report card. I don't understand. In fifth grade I did well. I have always done well in school.

Recess is my only escape from her. All the kids go to a field behind the church. It is off-limits, but the wire fence around it is falling in places, so it is easy to climb over it. Four trees grouped together make good shade.

We choose teams for our baseball games. No teachers, just kids from sixth to eighth grade having a ball game and some fun. One by one the captains choose their teams. Choosing teams and deciding who bats first sometimes takes all of first recess, so we return for lunch recess to actually play a game. Sometimes our games get really loud and we are chased off the forbidden field.

Sally and I eat our lunch on the steps of our classroom. The sun hits just right and warms up the cement steps. Sally's mom packs great lunches: a sandwich, Fritos, an apple, and a MoonPie. Sally shares her Fritos and MoonPie with me.

I like for us to eat just the two of us because many times at my house we have no bread for our sandwiches and have to use tortillas. Mom fills the freezer with bread, but sometimes we still run out. Bologna on a tortilla with mustard is good, but I am afraid kids will make fun of me. After lunch we often walk around talking and sometimes join our other friends.

Qué Bueno Que Se Acabo la Escuela

Summer vacation is just what I needed. Grampa sings our song, celebrating the fact that school is out. Grama and Grampa are always happy to have me.

I know what is expected of me here. Days do not change much. We spend our time cooking, cleaning, working the fields, visiting, and going to church. We play cards, checkers, Wajo, and I listen to Grampa's stories and riddles. Every meal is like a celebration, a coming together to enjoy each other and our food. Shortly after nightfall we rest and dream.

Eloy is in Germany with the army, and Viola is in Massachusetts getting ready for college at Our Lady of the Elms. She went early to meet the family she will be living with for four years. But the house is not empty—it is full with Grama and Grampa and me.

My stay in Mora this year was one short month. I am getting used to having to come back to Corrales. Sometimes I even look forward to it.

Back in Corrales, dew drops cover the earth. The smells of damp dirt and alfalfa blooming greet us at the five o'clock hour every morning. It is time to grab our hoes and whack the weeds out of the chile fields. It is important to mound airy dirt around the plants and cut away the choking morning glory vines and Johnson grass.

Tony and I race like always, trying to beat our record number of rows in one morning and seeing which of us hoes the most. Birds tweet and hide in the cottonwood trees. By the time we get home, Mom has breakfast ready. After breakfast we have our indoor chores, and then we are released from the bondage of work and turned loose to play. The neighborhood kids come to our house to play baseball, basketball, red rover, jacks, jump rope, and even to eat lunch with us. When the sun goes down and until dark, we return to the garden. After dark our friends return.

The two-acre cornfield has grown past needing to be hoed. Soon we will be picking, freezing, drying, and selling corn. After the corn we will pick apples, peaches, and vegetables and help Mom can and make jelly. We sell, roast, peel, freeze, and dry green chile, then pick, tie into *ristras*, grind into powder, and sell red chile.

Dad's dream to farm has come to fruition. Mom has been his biggest help. She can run the house and the outdoor chores. She puts us to work but leads by example. We as a family have all helped fulfill Dad's vision. Mom and Dad are hardworking teachers who led us with patience while we grew up enough to be of any real help.

Sally comes to my house and I go to hers. My responsibilities come first; then I am free to spend time with her. She usually helps me with my chores. Going to her house is like being on vacation. I don't have to help make breakfast, lunch, or dinner. I don't have to wash dishes, sweep the kitchen, or wash the floor. I get a break from cleaning house or hoeing the garden. She only has two chores every day: cutting up potatoes that her mother peels and cooks and cleaning one bathroom. Her sister is in charge of the other bathroom. After chores, we swim at the ditch and play with her sisters and visit her friends in the neighborhood. We eat snacks in front of the TV and talk for hours into the night.

Seventh Grade

My friends and I hugged and giggled our first day of school. We talked about our summers and all the new things that are happening in our lives, like how I found out recently that Mom is expecting another baby. The archbishop was at our church on Sunday and blessed Mom. She wants to name the new baby Edwin if it's a boy and Edwina if it's a girl, to honor Archbishop Edwin Vincent Byrne.

Mom wears those funny skirts with a hole cut out for her belly. Her blouses are now fitting tight. Uncle Juan warned her to wear keys on the tie over that hole in her skirt when there is a full moon. He said that if she doesn't, the baby can be born early during the full moon and not on the due date. Mom doesn't believe in superstitions, but I wonder if she'll do it just in case.

My friends are more interested in talking about boys and changes in their bodies and those kinds of things.

Every year more and more students leave Our Lady of Sorrows, but this year we also have three new students: Tony, my brother, Rosina, and Patty.

I already like Sister Godfrey. She walks and stands really straight. Sally named her Sister Robot, and sometimes we call her Sister Godfart, but I do really like her. I know exactly what she expects of me, and I like the way she teaches English grammar and how to break sentences into diagrams. The books she assigns to read become some of my favorites. She is fair and likes us.

My grades are back up. I am feeling good about school again. Sally and I hang around with Patty and Rosina most of the time. Patty is Sally's neighbor and sometimes when I go to Sally's house, we visit Patty or she comes to visit us.

The other day a bunch of girls were gathered around Father Sandoval, laughing because he teased Sally. All the girls think he is cute. I guess he is, but I don't find hanging around him to be much fun. I do it only because of the others. Father Baca came out of the rectory and sternly ordered us to leave Father Sandoval alone. "If you don't have anything better to do, go clean the bus."

He brought a bucket of water, a broom, and some rags and told us what to do. I climbed on the hood of the humongous bus and cleaned the windshield. It did not feel like a punishment to me because a whole group of my friends worked together, but Patty was feeling bad about it. To her it was humiliating. I guess I am used to it. Sharing work with friends is much easier than doing it alone.

San Ysidro Church

Mom and Dad talk about things that are happening all over Corrales at the dinner table. Dad talks about things he hears from the farmers, and Mom reports on what she hears from her church friends. After we eat, we all sit around talking some more. Us kids just talk about what is going on at school.

Rupert Lopez is mayordomo again. During his first term in 1941, he discovered that some adobe walls in the church were cracking. He and other people realized it was time to build a new church, and they made a commitment to save money from the fiestas.

Mom mentions to Dad, "Rupert wants to start building the new church."

"Is there enough money?" Dad asks.

"Jose Felipe Montoya, the treasurer of the church council, says that there is enough money saved. They can start construction."

Dad serves himself more beans and chile. "Rupert dropped by this afternoon to borrow my implements for the tractor. He is plowing and making rows for his *huerta*. He talked about the fiestas. He wants them to be a big hit and expects to make big money with the raffle."

"I have raffle tickets to sell. All the Catholic Daughters will be selling at least a book of ten. First prize is that calf you raised for the church."

"Yeah, Rupert asked me about the calf Koontz donated. I told him it is getting fat and ready. In fact, I bought ten dollars worth of raffle tickets from him."

"Why did you do that? I have to sell some too."

"I thought I'd help him out."

Friday evening many attend *vísperas*, vespers that start the San Ysidro fiestas. Our church is decorated in fresh May flowers and is full of believers. Guitars play and people sing in Spanish to San Ysidro Labrador. A bonfire lights our procession around the church as we follow the men carrying the decorated

La Fiesta procession, circa 1980s. Photo courtesy of Gloria Zamora.

statue. San Ysidro, the patron saint of farmers, is known to have been a good man. He was ordinary like the farmers in Corrales. He prayed every day and his wife, Maria Torribia, was a prayerful woman too. The priest said that she is known as Santa Maria de la Cabeza. Legend has it that an angel did San Ysidro's work while he spent hours praying. Farmers sometimes say in gratitude, "San Ysidro sent us rain."

Midmorning Saturday, we walk to Perea Hall to find Mom and other women making enchiladas, burritos, posole, and chile. People follow the smell of sopapillas frying in pans over open fires and come to eat fiesta food. Cooking over flames in booths is difficult but managed well by the Catholic Daughters and other parish women. Water is brought over from Florinda Lopez's house because the hall has no plumbing. Warming water over open fires and washing dishes in large washtubs is hard too. The red chile dirties the water, so the dishes are rinsed in a tub of water before washing them in the soapy water.

The whole community is involved in some way. Some people brought hand-sewn aprons and pillowcases, crocheted potholders, baked goods, homemade jelly, used books, toys, kitchen utensils, and other little *cositas* for the rummage sale. The money will all go to the fund for building the new church.

The Pereas' Tijuana Bar across the street is convenient for those who wish to have a beer or wine.

My sisters, our friends, and I go from inside the hall to the booths. We walk in the field behind the hall, then return to the booths for punch. We walk to the little store and back. Our mothers, busy cooking and selling food, tell us to come show our faces every once in a while to assure them that we are not misbehaving or missing in action.

Rupert Lopez serves as chairman of the building committee. Father Rutowski, pastor of Nativity Parish in Alameda, asked for monies from the San Ysidro savings during Mass one Sunday. People gasped and little whispers filled the church before a shocked silence took hold. They worry that he will get what has been saved for years and there will be no new church. San Ysidro is now a mission church belonging to the Nativity parish district, instead of Our Lady of Sorrows in Bernalillo. Rumor has it that Father Rutowski is using the money.

"It is only a rumor," Rupert tells those who gather around outside of the church. "I have no intention of turning any of the savings over to Father Rutowski, and I told him so."

A woman talking to Rupert exclaims, "Didn't you hear him during Mass? He plans to take our money!"

Rupert pats her arm. "I told him it is not our money. You know, mine and Jose Felipe's. It is the people's money."

"Still," she says, "I don't trust the man."

Rupert replies calmly, "It looks like Jose Felipe and I have to get people together and explain. I'll call you to come to the meeting. Okay?"

Rupert calls a large meeting to show bankbooks and to prove that no money has been deducted from the balance. The committee hopes to assure San Ysidro parishioners that their money is safe and that there is no truth to the rumors.

Land for the new church was acquired from a Mr. Gutierrez, who no longer lives in Corrales. Christino Griego offered to sell more property to the south, but it was not purchased.

Dad asked Rupert, "How large should the new building be?"

Rupert took a moment to consider the question. "I think the new church should hold at least two hundred people. That ought to be enough."

Rupert makes a chart to organize which volunteers will work what days. Many Corraleños help build their new church. Mr. Sena from Bernalillo Blocks has volunteered to teach men in Corrales how to lay block. Many already have built homes, and others will meet on Saturday to learn.

During Mass on Sunday, Father Rutowski has very nice things to say about the men who showed up to learn and those who showed up to teach. He makes sure to mention individuals by name. "Thank you all for coming Saturday and for volunteering to lay block. For the grace of God, these and other men will offer time and talents for the good of our parish. Let's give them a hand to show our gratitude."

The people clap and feel proud to be a part of such a big project.

Dad and Mom discuss the progress of the new church during many dinners. "Father Baca brought some windows from the church in Bernalillo," Mom says, and then muses, "I wish we were still part of Our Lady of Sorrows parish and that Father Baca was still our priest."

Father Baca was loved by the people in Corrales and it was hard to let him go.

"Teófilo Perea donated windows too. And all the Stations of the Cross. I hear Felipe Lucero Sr. will install heaters."

Mom interjects, "Oh, I thought Ignacio Perea did the plumbing and heating."

"Maybe so," Dad says. "Fred Martinez put up the ceiling."

Mom asks, "Who's in charge of the electricity?"

"The electrical work was hired out, I think."

Mom clicks her tongue in disappointment. "I thought they would use the pews from the old church, but they are selling them to raise money for new ones. Mathilda and Felice both bought one. I was too late and didn't get one."

"The off-white pews made of pressed wood are the best money can buy for the time being," Rupert told Mom one Sunday. "They look beautiful in the brand-new church."

San Ysidro parishioners are very proud of their church. Now it is finally a parish and not just a mission church. Father Tito Melendez is our first parish priest. He is Grampa's first cousin. They grew up together in Mora. Father Tito will live at Sylvia Montaño's little guesthouse until the rectory is completed.

Mom says, "If you can call it a guesthouse. It is a small adobe room that is falling down. It is more like a guest shack."

Catholic Daughters of the Americas

M embers of the Catholic Daughters of the Americas, known also as the Catholic Daughters and CDA, no longer meet in Mom's back room; now meetings are held at the just built San Ysidro parish hall.

My mother and her friends, Mathilda Palladini and Felice Heffenger, cook meals for the men building the fire department. The three of them volunteer for many committees all over Corrales. They teach catechism too. The volunteer work they do is not new, but now they work under the name of the Catholic Daughters.

CDA members have fund-raisers for charities and for people in need in the community. They have baby showers for unwed mothers, make baptismal bibs for babies, and serve breakfast to the families of the First Holy Communion children. They cook meals for the bereaved families in the parish. The other day they gathered clothes and groceries for a family that had a fire and everything in their house burned down. They donate money to charities around the world too. And CDA members use raised money to rent a bus for the Catholic Youth Organization members to use to attend retreats. I like when they send our CYO members on retreats to the Dominican Retreat House in Albuquerque.

We have a Mass and after Mass, a nice dinner. During the last part of dinner we listen to a priest or Sister give a talk and we reflect on the talk during our quiet time. We can go to confession if we want to. A bell tells us to gather together again to discuss what we thought about the evening retreat. We sing hymns accompanied by a guitar and get ready to go home. We arrive at the retreat house at six in the evening and leave at nine.

I feel at peace when I am at the Dominican Retreat House. During Mass, with the lights turned down and only candles lighting the altar, we can see the city from the chapel windows. Beautiful music plays quietly and fills the room with wonder. I feel like I am suspended in the sky, looking down at the twinkling city lights. Harps play in my heart and my feet reach

Catholic Daughters of the Americas, circa 1970. Left to right: Madeline Burlbaw, Dulcelina Curtis, and Luz Moreno. Photo courtesy of Gloria Zamora.

for holy ground. God is very present. I feel the love in each of us. I wish I could feel like this all the time.

The Catholic Daughters are having a Harvest Dinner. They decided at one of their meetings to use the harvest for a fund-raiser. There is always an abundance of chile, onions, tomatoes, pumpkins, and apples at the end of September. They voted to have a dinner on the first Sunday in October. Enchiladas, beans, Spanish rice, homemade tortillas, and sopa, sweet rice, and natillas for dessert are on the menu for this first Harvest Dinner.

People drive through Corrales on Sundays to get away from the city. Some come to buy locally grown produce. Today the Catholic Daughters hope the big signs will attract a large number of the cruisers to their Harvest Dinner.

My sisters and I have been recruited to help with the Harvest Dinner tomorrow. We are helping to set up tables and chairs, sweep and mop, and decorate the tables with centerpieces of colored corn and squash donated by Ida

Gutierrez. Luz Moreno has made candleholders from vegetable and coffee cans. She took snips and made fancy curly cues. They are beautiful. Every table has one on each end and has two saltshakers apiece, separated by the centerpiece.

Preparations began early this morning in homes across Corrales. Women are walking in with cookies, cupcakes, cakes, pies, and tortillas by the dozen. Refugio C de Baca and Rosario Lovato each brought several pans of sopa, toasted bread mixed with raisins, cinnamon, and cheese and soaked in a caramelized sugar syrup, then baked. Betty Reed and Mrs. Palladini put the beans in large roasters to cook early this morning. My mother, Irene Tafoya, and Lucy Martinez carried in gallon containers full of red chile already blended and cooked. Margarette Lucero is scheduled to bring more blended red chile later. Christine Sierra has cut and cooked pork to add to the red chile. The refrigerator has containers of shredded cheddar cheese donated by El Pinto, the restaurant where Lucy Martinez works. Lucy is frying corn tortillas. Using tongs, she dips several corn tortillas at once into heated oil and then wraps them in a wet kitchen towel to keep them soft. Betty, Mom, and Felice are dicing onions and lettuce.

Consuelo Pedroncelli and Sylvia Montaño are to take the money for the bake sale. Mom has asked my sisters and me to bus tables, waitress, and wash dishes.

People are lined up at the door all the way outside. Mass just let out and it looks like the whole congregation decided to come and eat. First they pay Elvira Modica, get a meal ticket, and come to the window for the enchilada plate. Felice Heffinger takes the ticket and informs the cooks if there are any special instructions and how many plates go with the order. Mom, Betty Reed, and Lillian Chavez serve food onto the plates and place them on the counter next to Felice. She has my sisters and me take the orders to the tables. This shift will work for two hours until the second set of members replace us, and a third will come in later.

Drinks are set up where the customers can serve themselves. They can choose coffee or tea or apple cider, which Dulcelina Curtis has donated.

As fast as we wash dishes they are used again to serve new customers. The large crowd enjoys the live entertainment and the food. The baked goods are selling fast.

The dinner is from eleven to five o'clock. CDA members come and work for two hours, then leave. Some will return for their pots and pans and to help clean up. Just as some women were assigned to the set-up crew, others are assigned to the clean-up crew. Mom says we are coming back later to help clean up.

The clean-up crew folds up tables and chairs, gathers centerpieces, and washes the stove, sinks, and floors, leaving the hall exactly like we found it. Mathilda teases, "Thank God for the Catholic sons, the husbands, who come to help."

Elvira Modica, the treasurer, is counting money. She hollers to get our attention, "Everybody listen!" Sweeping, mopping, and the clanging of pots and pans all stop. "We made a grand profit. After deducting expenses, we came out twelve hundred dollars ahead."

Everybody cheers.

It is dark and late when the lights are turned off. Doors are locked and workers already planning next year's Harvest Dinner get into cars to drive home. Working side by side with all of Mom's friends has been fun. It feels good to have been part of this day. I have learned that volunteering is giving back to the Lord, and that we gain so much from our work. I think my religion instructors and Mom are right.

Warmth in Snow-Covered Mountains

In winter the mountains are covered in snow. It is just like that on our drive to Las Aguitas for Thanksgiving. Thanksgiving means three families gather together under Grama's roof. One roof with only four rooms, and one of these is reserved for Mom and Dad, even though it is usually saved for special company, company that is served coffee and stays only a little while. They sit on the sofa, sofa arms covered with doilies, doilies that Grama crochets at night before going to bed, sitting in her rocking chair, whistling and humming.

Cold winter nights mean darkness and sleeping until we wake when the sun rises over the mountain. Grampa lights a fire and warms the house. The house is warm before anyone else leaves the comfort of blankets. Comforting is the four-room house where we spend Thanksgiving each year.

We're on the way to Grama's house. We sing, "Over the river and through the woods, to Grandmother's house we go," several times. We have been on the road for almost two hours.

In Las Vegas Dad stops at the side of the road and puts chains on the tires. Tony helps. We might make it to Grama's house in an hour or less, depending on the roads.

When we turn onto the quarter-mile driveway through Grampa's property to get to the house, I notice light from the kitchen window. The road winds and I lose sight of the light, then it reappears. Usually black darkness surrounds us, but tonight absolute whiteness envelops sky and earth, lighting brushy limbs burdened with snow, pine tree branches leaning, nearly touching the ground. Snowcapped fence posts guide us on our unseen path. The pitch of Grama's farmhouse reveals smoke weaving through the sky.

Dad slows to a turtle pace before taking the driveway downward to the house. Standing at the open door, Grama's silhouette is waiting. Before the

Left to right, back row: Fidel Valdez, Ninfa Valdez, and Tomas Tafoya; left to right, middle row: Tony Tafoya, Dolores Tafoya, Viola Martinez, Gloria Tafoya, Irene Tafoya; front row, left to right: Diana Tafoya, Mark Tafoya, Lucille Valdez, Joseph Tafoya, Lulu Valdez holding Elizabeth Valdez. Photo courtesy of Fidel Valdez Jr.

station wagon engine comes to a complete halt, we run and plow into her. Her belly shakes with pure joy and laughter. Grampa joins the huddle and arms are reaching and grabbing for him. We share group hugs and kisses.

Grama insists we eat. "I'll build up the fire and warm the food."

Before anything else I run to the cupboard and grab bizcochitos. The kitchen smells like pumpkin pie. At least six pies covered with towels sit on the shelf behind the screen.

We talk into the night. Then the mattresses are pulled off the beds and are spread from wall to wall, colchones everywhere. We try not to step on each other's heads or bodies, but if we do, laughter is sure to start on one side of the room and spread to the other. That we ever fall asleep is miraculous. Grama loves it. The adults turn out the lights and tell us to hush and go to sleep.

By tomorrow night not only the six of us will be on the floor, but also an additional bunch of Uncle Benny's kids, and they are a bunch.

We're up early. Who can sleep? The mattresses are put back on the beds and Grama is making oatmeal for breakfast.

Playing in the snow, slipping and sliding we laugh and scream.

Two hens and a rooster barely fit in the roaster. Tío Facundo has come to join us for our Thanksgiving meal. He prays and prays and goes on praying. He thanks the Lord for every little thing he can think of. Finally we start to eat. The men are served first, and then the kids, and by the time Grama and Mom sit to eat, we are out in the snow, sliding down the mountain.

Roasting piñon is my favorite smell. Grampa poured handfuls of piñon in a cast-iron pan and put it in the oven. Flames come up to meet kindling he hurls into the orange-yellow blaze. It may be two degrees below zero outside, but around the kitchen table it is cozy.

Every time Grampa stirs the nuts I hope they are ready to eat. He gives us all a sample to try. To me, the less piñon is cooked the better. Everyone has an opinion about when piñon is cooked just right.

Grampa plays cards with Dolores, Diana, and me. Dad plays checkers with Tony, and Mom and Grama talk in the other room. Mark and Joseph are playing with cap guns and running around the house. Edwina constantly sleeps like month-old babies do. Uncle Benny and my cousins went to visit Aunt Mary and will be back later to sleep.

Little piles of piñon shells accumulate around the table. Grampa cracks his piñon with the saltshaker. He says the dentures just don't work. Once in a while he passes me a few shelled nuts and I toss them in my mouth. My sisters say I am spoiled, and I feel like I have to explain. "He always cracks them for me. It started when I was little and he just stayed in the habit."

Grama and Mom are pulling mattresses off the beds. We have finished our Rummy game, had our fill of piñon, and our cousins are back. Tonight there are even more mattresses spread on the floor. The boys sleep in one room and the girls in the other. We girls giggle and the boys wrestle until Mom and Grama turn out the lights.

Uncle Benny and his family leave after breakfast. I'm going to read for a little while. Grampa set up the game of Wajo for whoever wants to play. He and Dad are taking off to the mountain to see if they can find any deer or other wildlife.

It is one of those very dark nights and Grampa calls out to us over the noise, "I am roasting apples. Who wants apples?" In a few quick minutes all of us are gathered in the back bedroom, sitting on rugs that Grama made. The adults are sitting on the beds, even though we are not allowed to sit on them during the day. Grampa starts one of those stories about a witch carrying one of us away to a distant place. The suspense is too much for the younger kids like Mark and Joseph. I can see they are falling for every word. I am used to hearing these stories from Tío Manuel and sometimes Tío Miguel. Grampa is not as spooky as they are.

Smelling burnt caramel beads of bubbly apple juice making popping and hissing sounds as they skip atop the two-burner stove distracts me from the story. Grampa stops to turn the apples so they will roast evenly, then he sticks his finger in his mouth. I can hardly wait to suck warm sweet apple bites right down to the core.

Grampa starts up with the riddles. Now Tony listens and gets into them. When I try telling the same riddles, he blows me off. Dolores and I are puzzled and try hard to figure them out. Grampa loves to challenge even Dad. We laugh, sigh, gasp, and munch our apples. I love this night.

After Sunday Mass we eat a late breakfast and pack our bags. We will leave before dark. I keep leaning on Grama and holding her arm or her hand. She has the softest hands. I follow her from one room to the other. I touch her hair and put my arm around her shoulder. I am never ready to leave Grama or Grampa.

Good-byes are hard on Grama, Mom, and me. Grama cries as we pull away and Mom and I cry in the car. Once we are out of Mora, we are singing songs with the rest of the family. Dad sings, "I'm going to leave," and we repeat the words. Then he sings "For Texas now," and we echo. We sing many songs: "My Bonny Lies over the Ocean"; "Ain't Gonna Grieve My Lord No More"; "Oh My Darling Clementine"; "You Are My Sunshine"; "On Top of Old Smokey"; and many more.

Tied to the top of our station wagon is a Christmas tree Dad and Grampa cut from the forest. When we get home Dad will put it in a bucket with water. We will have to wait two weeks before we decorate it.

Big snowflakes begin to fall as quiet as cotton balls. Dad has a hard time seeing the road. He does not stop for gas in Las Vegas like Mom has practically ordered him to. We are between Pecos and Santa Fe when the car sputters and Dad pulls over to the shoulder. It is cold and dark.

Tony and Dad hitchhike to Santa Fe to get gas for the car. Mom has us lock our doors and an unspoken order to be quiet is understood. I fall asleep and am awakened when Tony and Dad are refueling. We stop in Santa Fe and fill up the car with gasoline.

Once home, all is well. Snow covers the ground in Corrales and we have school in the morning. It is time to go to bed.

This Little Piggy

We are getting ready for a *matanza*. Dad has built a fire and warmed two large fifty-five-gallon containers of water and constructed a place to set the hog after it has been killed. Mom is getting buckets and pots and pans ready. Knives have been sharpened and Dad makes scrapers for us kids to use by folding the lids of tin cans in half. We hold the folded end and the sharp edges scrape off the pig's hair.

Dad is trying to show Tony where to shoot the pig. The pig is squealing and running all over the pen. Finally Dad does the pig a favor, and with one shot kills the poor animal. The pig is very heavy, but Tony and Dad manage to drag it like an altar offering onto a table made of two by fours.

Once on the table, its blood is drained. Dad cuts right down the center and removes the tripe, liver, heart, kidneys, and all stomach parts, throwing away the *pajarería*.

Dad adds lye to the heated water, which bubbles ferociously. He fills a bucket with boiling water and pours it on the sacrificial pig, who still sports a long thin smile across a protruded snout and pink nostrils as though happy to oblige.

We step back while more buckets of boiling water are poured over the carcass. We laugh and talk like there is a party going on. We are ready to pounce with our sharp weaponry upon the unwanted hair. It falls to the ground in little piles. It surprises me that we are so excited about this work. We enjoy working together.

Skinned to a whitish pink, the pig, clean of all its hair, lies before many inspecting eyes. Then Tony scrapes the curly tail clean, and Dad cuts the tail and puts it in the hot coals from the burning fire, now just a place to warm our hands and bodies. He places the liver on rocks over the coals too.

We say our prayer of thanksgiving at the table before we eat fresh tortillas, red chile, pinto beans, fried potatoes, crispy liver, and fried pork.

Mom cooks the head in the oven for dinner. In a few weeks we'll use pork for making tamales, posole, and *empanaditas* to serve on Christmas Eve.

Dad divides the pig into quarters and hangs them in the walk-in cooler. He will take a quarter at a time and cut up the meat into pork chops, steaks, roasts, and ribs. But first he cuts strips of *lonja*, the fat, into small pieces and fries them in the *perol*, a large copper kettle he inherited from Great-grandma Trinidad. He renders the fat and makes *chicharrones*, crisp meaty cracklings, to eat with tortillas.

Santa Claus Is Coming to Town

Dad takes us to see Christmas lights all over the North Valley. We ooh and aah at every house, suggesting this one is better than the last one. All are beautiful and we could do this all night. Other cars line up on the streets, our paths lit only with Christmas lights. Nine of us sit in the car singing "Silent Night," "Jingle Bells," and other traditional Christmas songs on the way to Atrisco. Even Edwina, the baby, sings a word here and there.

Back at our house, dozens of lit luminarias line the road from our neighbor's house all the way to ours and around our driveway. They will burn through midnight and some will remain lit until morning, but we will not be back to see them.

Dad drives on some ditchbanks, taking a shortcut to Grandma Patrocinia's house. I don't remember using this route before. In Grandma Patrocinia's neighborhood luminarias illuminate paths to front doors and on sidewalks. When we arrive, our hugs and kisses are received, and after a short visit with Aunt Corina, Aunt Bea, and my grandparents, it is time to go to bed. We have to sleep now and get up later for midnight Mass.

Grandma Patrocinia's Christmas tree has many presents under it. When we left Corrales, our tree had no presents underneath it. Mom and Dad told us Santa Claus would come while we are in Atrisco, because Mark, Joseph, and Edwina still believe in Santa. In reality, Tony and Dad put the presents under the tree while we waited for Dad in the car. Mom made it more real by honking the horn like she always does when Dad is slow and late. Only this time when Dad got in the car, she only pretended to be mad. He reached over, pinched her chin, and said, "*No te enojes, mi* hōney." Honey has a long "o" like in Tony. That is what they call each other.

Daddy retold the Santa Claus story we hear every year. "We took you kids to the Christmas parade downtown when you were very little. Santa Claus was throwing candy to all the people on the sidelines. No candy fell by us, so Tony made sure Santa knew where he stood. He waved and called out, '*Santo Clos, aquí estoy yo. Santo Clos.*'"

I love to hear about when Tony was younger, and I always want to hear more. Dad must have read my mind. "Tony didn't like the dark. One time we were walking to Mamá's. Tony was about two. I hadn't taken a flashlight. Tony looked around and put his hands on his hips. Pretending to be brave, he said, '*Está curo*, Daddy.'"

We all laughed. Dad remembers a lot about Tony. Even Tony laughs at how cute he was. "Remember how I said 'happy nee nee' for 'happy new year'?"

"Yes, Tony, we sure do remember," Daddy assured him.

I can't wait to see what is under our tree, but first we will go to midnight Mass. After church we will return to Grandma's and open presents, eat posole, tamales, empanaditas, bizcochitos, and pastelitos. We'll get home about two thirty in the morning, but no matter how tired we are, we'll open our presents before going to bed.

I know what some of the gifts are because Mom gave each of us five dollars to spend on each other. Boys buy boys' gifts and girls buy girls'. I bought Dolores a new diary and Diana a new jump rope. I wrapped them immediately so they would not be discovered. Diana can't help herself; she snoops until she knows what all her presents are. But I hid the one I bought well, so she'll at least have that surprise. Myself, I love surprises on Christmas.

So Long Seventh, Hello Eighth Grade

I am going to miss "Sister Godfrey Gordon Gustavus Gore, why don't you think to shut the door?" Sally renamed her after having to memorize the poem. I wonder if Sister Godfrey heard Sally calling her other names? Anyway, she is the best teacher I have had at Our Lady of Sorrows School. There were some times when I thought she could mind her own business, but I realize she is good-hearted and wishing only the best for me.

I love the way Cher wears her hair. I now wear long straight bangs that cover my eyebrows. Sometimes I iron my hair or I have Dolores iron my hair. My hair is straight, but I want it to be even straighter. Mom let me wear mascara and eyeliner this year too. I feel pretty good about the way I look except I wish Mom would allow me to shave my legs and pluck my eyebrows. Our uniforms are still green-checkered jumpers, and we wear white blouses under them and beanies when we go to Mass, but that is okay. I do my best to look like Cher.

Sister Godfrey has sent a couple of notes home to Mom about the long bangs. She is afraid I will go blind or at least cross-eyed with such interference to my sight. Mom lectured me for a while after the notes came home, but then forgot and never made me cut my bangs.

As far as eighth grade goes, I heard that Sister Sylvan is tough. Those who go to the principal's office say she is harsh.

Only eight girls and five boys returned to Our Lady of Sorrows for eighth grade. My brother, Tony, refused to come back after giving it a try. Annie and Geraldine and some of the other girls have boyfriends now, so I make up this story that I met a boy in Mora this summer. I tell them Freddy and I kissed, that we plan to write letters to each other, and that he writes that he really likes me. My lie gets bigger and bigger. I don't think they will ever figure out that Freddy is my aunt's nephew. I even say his last name and tell them that he is from Pecos. I exaggerate about his green eyes and his light complexion, which are his features, but I make him out to be as handsome as Fabian or Bobby Dean.

I never thought my lie would catch up to me, but it did. Annie told a friend of hers and that friend is Freddy's cousin. Annie said, "Freddy said he is not your boyfriend and he is not writing you letters."

I know my whole face revealed that I had been caught, but I tried hard to hide it. "He lies, or your friend lies."

"Show me one of the letters he wrote to you."

"I will!"

For days I kept telling her and the other girls that I forgot the letters. Finally I had to admit to Sally that I had lied. I wanted to cry. I thought my year was spoiled and that my schoolmates would never like me again.

Sally said, "Why did you lie? Darn you. Here I was all green with envy. I really believed you. Don't worry about telling them the truth. Annie is being mean, anyway. She likes to make you sweat."

I decided that day after talking to Sally that I would never again make up stupid stories or tell lies. It felt good to get the lie off my chest, thanks to Sally.

Sister Sylvan, it turns out, loves me, and I love her too. She is about five foot five, wears a wrinkled habit, and slumps in her chair and falls asleep at her desk. If ever there is an opposite of Sister Godfrey in neatness, it is Sister Sylvan. We make fun of her while she sleeps and take advantage writing and passing notes. Sometimes she pulls out a small mirror, hides it behind a book pretending to read, and pulls out little white whiskers from her chin.

The first time I saw her pull whiskers, I went home and asked Dolores if Sister Sylvan did it when she was her teacher. "Oh yes. I think they grew all week and on Fridays she would pluck or shave. She always fell asleep too. In fact, one time the whole class stood up in unison, saluted, and said, 'Heil Hitler.' And that is how we woke her."

"Whoa, she hates Hitler, why'd you do that? I can just see it. Did she punish you guys for it?"

"She went into her long speech about how the communists are burning all the churches in Russia and how people are sacrificing their lives for Jesus."

"I know what you mean. She asked us if we are ready to be martyrs for

Christ and for our faith. I don't think I'd make it in those countries. She is crazy to ask, really. Don't you think?"

"Gloria, you have to be ready to give up your life for Jesus. He gave his life for us. I think I would die for Jesus."

"You go right ahead. Not me, thank you."

Dolores takes many things the nuns say too seriously. I have to remember not to talk to her about martyrdom.

Principal's Pet

S ister Sylvan sends me to take over the first-grade class when that teacher has to run errands or take someone home or to the doctor. My little brother Joseph is in that class. He is the smartest first-grade student. I like writing on the board and asking questions. One time I was in charge through the morning. When recess came, I saw little girls chasing Joseph. He hates that.

Sometimes Sister sends both Sally and me. She knows we are best friends and does not punish us for it like Sister Rosine Marie used to. Thank God I don't have *Roscina* for my teacher anymore. I know I should not call a nun an anus, but I can't help myself. When I see her walk by, I dream up revenge like sending her *rosca* to the North Pole to freeze her royal hiney, but most of the time I don't think about her at all.

Sister Sylvan is so good. I can see that she really loves God. She is not just saying words that are written in prayer books; she says really fine words to God when we pray before our religion class, like she is talking to her best friend.

This year Father Baca is having us read the whole Bible. It is so hard to understand and some of the words are extremely difficult to pronounce, but we go up and down the rows, taking turns reading the Bible every day.

Today Father Baca was pretty angry. I lost interest in the Bible reading and was laughing at something Sally said. He said to me, "Would you like to share with the rest of us what is so funny, Tafoya?" Whoa. He has never talked to me like that. I remained in my seat and kept quiet. "Stand when you are addressing me." I stood. I knew my answer would get Sally into trouble. My silence bordered on disrespect and disobedience. He finally said, "Sit down. Next time you will not get off so easy."

Since last year Sally and I have had crushes on two of our classmates. Our secret names for them are George and Ringo, after our favorite Beatles.

We have spelling and math bees. The girls line up on one side of the room and the boys on the other. Robert and I are always up at the end. Sister will end the bee if the bell rings or if the hour is over. She gives us holy cards for staying up the longest. I have so many holy cards in my drawer at home. I smile at Robert and he smiles at me, and we won't let the other win. I love his green eyes. I think he knows it too. The main thing Robert is better at than me is his penmanship. He has the neatest writing and his numbers are small and line up in straight columns. My papers have eraser smudges all over them, and no matter how hard I try, my writing stinks.

Recently, Sally and I spoke like adults. I asked her why she liked Pat, and she said, "I don't know—he's kinda noble. He's really good looking too. I know all the girls have crushes on him, but it would be nice if he noticed me!"

My first boy-girl party has me wishing I had never committed to Sally or my other friends that I would come. Mom and Dad picked Sally up at her house, and now they are driving us to the party. Sally can't wait to get there. She helps Dad find the address on the house because it is dark.

In the car my parents tell Sally and me to be ready to leave at ten o'clock. Walking to the door, I can hear voices from inside. Sally is anxious to see who has come. I am anxious in a different way.

Dad follows Eppi's father into the den. Mom and his mother stay in the kitchen, drinking some punch. Eppi's mother tells Sally and me, "Go into the den. The party is in there."

Friends are standing around, talking and listening to music. Dad and Eppi's father sit in recliners right in the den. A few of our old classmates, the ones who do not attend Our Lady of Sorrows anymore, have come. It is as though they never left. Before long we are talking and dancing. I don't notice Dad and Mom. Sally and Pat dance a slow song. He holds her hand and stays by her and they talk for a short time. I am so happy for her. This end of the year party is so much fun. Robert talks to me, but doesn't dance with me or with anyone else. Most of the night he stands with the guys, and I never see him talk to another girl.

On our drive home Sally whispers, "I feel so special just that he asked me to dance. All the expectations, and then he asked! I was disappointed that he asked Marjorie first. He must know I like him. How could he not know?"

Eighth grade graduation is tomorrow. Our Lady of Sorrows has been a good experience. We have been told that our school will close its doors after this year. We all feel very sad about that. We will miss each other, and I will miss Sister Sylvan and Sister Godfrey.

I had been looking forward to high school on the other side of the road. The two-story building with an enclosed patio is a mystery to me. I have watched sophisticated boys and girls cross the street for four years. Girls looking like movie stars in beehive hairdos, pulling out hairspray and makeup to fix themselves up. Boys holding hands with girls, pulling out half-hidden combs from back pockets, making sure their Brylcreem hairdos are slicked back perfectly. I think that as the commercial says, "a little dab will do you," does not apply to them.

The only chance I ever got to cross to the high school building was when I worked washing dishes in the cafeteria to earn my lunch. I could hardly reach into the deep sinks. Many third through eighth-grade students were offered this opportunity, so I only went three times. The meals were delicious.

One of the biggest things that happened this year was when on a November day, all the students heard an extra bell ring. The bell would not stop ringing. To us it meant a fire drill. We all stopped playing on the playground and lined up to be counted. But instead of being counted by our teachers, Sister Sylvan stood up on the steps of our eighth-grade room and made an announcement. "Children, today is a sad day for our country. President John F. Kennedy has been assassinated. He was shot today, and he has died."

Everyone gasped and moaned at the same time. Sister Sylvan actually cried. "We must pray," she said. "Pray for his soul and for his family. Pray for our country." Her crying started a chain reaction. It began at one end of the schoolyard and went to the other end, and both teachers and students cried. President Kennedy was such a good president, according to my father and all our relatives and friends. At our house we heard so much about him, it was as if he was the best president after President Lincoln.

At the mention of our country, I thought about the many times Sister Sylvan talked about communism and churches being burned and sacrificing our lives for Jesus, and hearing my father talk of Russia and Khrushchev and Dad's little phrase, "The Ruskies are coming." And hearing Sister Sylvan's concerns, I couldn't help but think that our country was in some kind of danger.

That night I prayed about President Kennedy and I prayed for our country, and I decided not to worry about any of this anymore. But I couldn't help but worry because everyone, everywhere was talking about it. For weeks on the television news there were playbacks of the killing, the arrest, the country's grief, and the beautiful Catholic funeral. Everyone cried for President Kennedy. My dad said, "He will go down in history for being the best president who ever served our country."

I will never forget Andy Williams standing at the pulpit singing "Ave Maria" in a beautiful voice that brought the angels and the saints and the souls of the departed to our presence. I could tell Andy Williams mourned the loss of a good friend. I could tell that everyone attending the Mass felt the loss of a great man.

Today is our eighth-grade retreat. We will attend Mass, and Sister Sylvan is explaining what will happen after Mass. "You are expected to pray and keep silence all day. Reflect on what God is doing and has done in your life. You can give thanks for those gifts. You can also pray for any needs you have. For instance, I will pray today for my sister who is in the hospital. I want her to get well. My nieces are very worried about her. I also want to ask God to keep each of you safe for always.

"God is always present and ready to listen to your prayers. Talking to God silently or out loud is very natural and very comforting. Today is a day to think about all those beautiful things in your life you are grateful for. I will be thanking him for having had the opportunity to be your teacher and that I met you and that you are all such wonderful human beings and have a lot to offer to the world." She stopped to take a breath.

"I *am* proud of every one of you. Today Father Baca will talk with you a little bit; he'll offer a retreat talk and then you will be on your own. Stay on the grounds. If you meet up with a friend, you may smile at them, but do not exchange words. It will be hard because you are not used to doing that, but at the end of the day you will see how wonderful you will feel because you spent the whole day with God. Think about that!"

Sister Sylvan is walking us over to the church. She takes large steps. I think it is sad that our class will not be led to the church like this ever again. And I am really sad to leave such a woman of faith. Sister Sylvan really loves us. I am going to thank God for her.

The high school choir is singing for our eighth-grade retreat. Father Baca is dressed in his white shiny robes. Incense is burning. Mother Mary holds dead Jesus in her arms and looks so sad. Angels hang above the altar, looking down at us. It all feels so holy. Jesus also hangs nailed to the cross. Father holds the Host and offers the Mass for our benefit. Sister Sylvan sits next to us. She has her eyes closed and I think she must be talking to God right now. It is really holy. The Mass ends. The high school choir goes on back to class.

Father Baca has us sit in the church. He explains what we will do today and that it is a day for reflection. "Look into your souls and see if there are any sins you are sorry for. For an examination of conscience you pray and ask God to help you remember what sins you have committed. After you are aware of your sins, say a good act of contrition for them. Ask God to help you not to commit those sins ever again. After you think you are ready, I will hear confessions starting at one o'clock."

Father tells a story: "A boy and his father had to walk several miles through the desert to see a sick uncle. They had little time because the uncle was near death. The path was long and quiet. The hot sun beat down on them, and they were running out of water. The boy's father prayed they would make it on time to see his sick uncle. They jumped over walls, crawled under fences, and now they faced a large ravine. The father took a long leap and jumped to the other side. The ravine was deep and looked dangerous. The little boy was afraid. 'I can't make it,' he said. 'Yes, you can, son. Run back and take it at a run.' The boy did as his father instructed, but stopped himself right before reaching the edge. Father said to son, 'You have to cross here. We can go for miles before there is a better place to cross. It is too far to go back, and we don't have much time.' He knew the boy would get lost if he sent him back home alone. They were separated and the boy was scared. He had no choice but to try again. 'We are almost to our destination, son. Just jump, I'll catch you.' The boy finally jumped. His father caught him and said, 'I told you I would catch you.'"

Father Baca reflects, "He finally put his trust in the father. That is the kind of trust God asks us to put in him."

The story reminds me of the time my grandfather asked me to jump to him. We were up high on some tall boulders and he wanted me to jump to him. It took a long time and many promptings. I had to trust Grampa, and in the end I jumped. I remember feeling so good that I was able to do it, and that when it was all over, everything turned out just fine. I believe if I can trust anybody, it is God.

I keep silence the whole day. I examine my conscience and think about the other day when I was talking to Dolores about not being able to forgive Sister Rosine Marie for the way she treated me. I said to Dolores, "She failed me all the time. She made me feel like a total failure. Dang, I can't stand her. I wish she'd go to hell."

Dolores listened and hugged me while I cried. "You know what we can do. We can pray about it."

"I always pray, right before going to confession, but it doesn't help."

"Gloria," she said, "I have an idea. You save letters from Grama and you save letters from your friends. Did you save your report card from sixth grade?"

"Yeah. Why?"

"Bring your report card and we'll look at it and pray after looking at it."

"I don't want to look at that thing again. It will make me madder. I don't like your idea."

"Let's try it. You can't hate her more than you already do. And God can help you when you pray."

I brought the report card and we looked at it together. I smiled and put the report card into Dolores's face. "Look at this, only one F. All this time I thought she failed me in everything."

Dolores pulled my hand away from her face. "If she had failed you in everything, you wouldn't have passed to seventh grade."

"Oh, Dolo, I'm shocked. Forever I have felt so stupid, so dumb, and all because I thought she had failed me in everything."

"Do you want to pray?"

"I'm still mad at her. I'll have to pray really hard for many years, I think."

I go to confession and tell Father about feeling angry toward a teacher. I feel so clean. I talk to God all day, and when my mind wanders off to other things, I remind myself of today's purpose. I smile at friends I meet and keep walking. I ask God to help me not be afraid of my new school next year.

I am wearing a new white dress, high heels, and hose. Nylon stockings are so hard to put on. Mom showed me how to be careful and not put a hole or a run in them. Walking in high heels is tricky. If I don't concentrate, my feet wiggle under me. I feel pretty and grown-up. After Mass we are having a reception in the hall with all our families. Aunt Bea and Grandma Patrocinia have come to my graduation. I am proud of my school.

Sister Sylvan gave us each a present: a pearl-white rosary in a container shaped like a white graduation cap. One of my aunts gave me a charm bracelet made of white pearl beads. It is a decade of a rosary. I also received my first electric shaver so I will not go around with cut legs anymore. My happiest moment was seeing Grandma Patrocinia going up to communion. I loved having at least one of my grandparents at my graduation.

Nothing Lasts Forever

My parents always say, "Nothing lasts forever." They usually say that to me when I'm upset about changes in school or with friends. It bugs me when I hear it.

It's sad around our house. Grandpa Jesús has been in the hospital for three weeks now. Mom decided I should wait to go to Mora until he gets out of the hospital. She said, "If he gets out." I don't like the sound of that.

I have gone to the hospital to see him and he does not even know anyone is there. He moans "Ay" over and over again, expressing pain. He has gotten so skinny. Even his hair is thinning out more. I wish I could help him in some way.

On June sixteenth, death comes to our family. For years I have greeted Grandpa the minute I walk into his house. He sits in the recliner and hardly ever leaves it. He teases us with his cane by pulling us toward him or pushing us away. He pinches us when we pass by and gives us money to go to the little store for candy. Now the chair sits empty and we'll never again hear that little teasing laugh.

I have attended many funerals, but this one has my aunts and cousins crying, and all my sisters and brothers and I cry. Daddy cries and he hardly talks. He and Uncle Manny keep hugging and crying. I have gone around giving *pésame* to Grandma and every aunt and uncle. But I have not offered condolences to my dad. I find it hard to see him cry. I don't know if he has noticed or not, but I better go up to him and do it soon. It seems odd that I haven't.

Grandma Patrocinia is very quiet. When Grandpa Jesús died, she was at his side saying the rosary out loud. She seems to be at peace. Perhaps she is out of tears.

The Santa Clara cemetery is where Aunt Lilly is buried. Dad shows us her grave and where our baby, Mom's firstborn, is buried. There are other relatives buried here too. Grandpa will be in the company of family.

Dad keeps telling us stories about Grandpa. I know he loved his father very much. Bowing our heads, we pray the Lord's Prayer with the priest. Our last good-byes are personal. I touch the casket before it is lowered, and when it is on its way down, we all throw a handful of dirt on top. The desert heat doesn't seem to keep the chill away. I feel cold and sad.

Qué Bueno Que Se Acabo la Escuela

Mom finally let me come to Mora. Lucille has been here since school ended. I thank God Grama and Grampa are healthy and that I still have them.

Lucille is teaching me how to dance the "locomotive." All week we have been climbing ladders and trees, picking cherries, and dancing the locomotive. She says that I am bowlegged. "You stand with your legs together, and if they don't touch at the calves, you are bowlegged," she explains. She also says that I am not dancing right.

I am glad she is teaching me a new dance, but she reminds me of the time I didn't "doo ah doo" correctly for Sally when she and I sang "Do You Want to Know a Secret." She expected me to sing as well as the Beatles. Sally would not talk to me for days. She was so upset about it, she had some of the other girls ignoring me too.

Charlotte was the only girl brave enough to come around. She and I walked and talked and I told her how sad I felt about what was happening to me. She encouraged me to confront Sally. I became so distraught, I finally approached Sally. By this time I had forgotten exactly what had made her so angry, and she still was not ready to talk.

Later that day she wrote on the blackboard, "I'm sorry, Gloria, for being so mean to you." The fact that she went public with the apology struck me. In my eyes it saved me from all the humiliation I had suffered. The rest of the girls started to talk to me again, like I had suddenly become important. Sally apologized and explained everything. She actually admitted, "It was a stupid reason to get mad. I really missed you a lot."

Lucille and I are walking to the *lagunita*. Surrounded by mountains, not even the moon lights our way. I have the flashlight in my possession, or I would not have come. Once in a while I move the light to our left, then our right, and behind to make sure there are no surprises in the dark. Her transistor radio is tuned to KOMA out of Oklahoma. We can't reach any other radio station that plays our kind of music in these mountains.

We sit on the banks of the lagunita and listen to Wolfman Jack. I am not as comfortable sitting out here in the dark as Lucille is. The moon is finally peeking over the mountain peaks. Stars dot the sky like sugar sprinkles. Cool air chills my face and hands. The night air smells musty like warm baked clay.

Light comes from the direction of the house, bouncing from earth to sky and from north to south. Mumbling voices stretch across the distance. Grama and Grampa are coming toward us. I am delighted and want to run toward them. Lucille whispers, "What are they doing here?"

Lucille went back to Santa Fe earlier than the original plan. I am hanging out with Grampa in the fields. This year he decided to plow Tío Candido's land and plant a winter wheat. Ever since Grampa started using a tractor to plow and seed, he has found more time in the day to plant more.

Grama and I are visiting with Tía Mariana. I'm going outside, where Tío Oso is fixing the doghouse. I don't trust something about this dog. While the dog is busy watching Tío, I sneak to the field where Grampa goes round and round, crushing clumps of rocky dirt.

Crossing under a barbed-wire fence, I look back at Tío's house. I can only see the pitch of the roof. Grampa is a few hundred yards from me. Each footstep I take sinks into the freshly cut dirt. Suddenly I hear a loud growl and turn quickly. At my heels is Tío's half dog, half wolf. I run but my feet feel heavy and I can't move in the plowed soil. I scream for Grampa. Though he hears me and sees my waving hands and stops the tractor, he does not move toward me.

Instead, he yells, "Don't run! He'll chase you if you run. You have to stop running." I hear the words but I don't believe him. The dog is right at my heels, growling and barking and ready to take a chunk out of me.

I am crying now and very angry that Grampa is not helping me. I run as best I can, but I trip and fall. My face is covered in dirt. I bury it in my hands to protect myself from the dog's bite. The bite never happens. Grampa is right. The chase is over. I guess if the dog wanted a chunk of flesh, he would have taken it.

Part III

| *1966–1967* |

Back to Public School

Taylor Middle School takes some getting used to. There are three lunch times and it is up to me to know which one is mine. There are teachers for each subject and I have to find them before a late bell rings. Science is in a separate part of the building than English and so on. My first day has finally passed, and I stressed about being late all day, but I made it just fine.

I have no classes, or lunch, with Sally and have to make new friends to have lunch with. In fourth period I look around to see if I know anyone. To my distress, not one person looks familiar. Eating alone is not an option, and the girl to my left looks friendly, so I speak to her and ask if I can join her for lunch. The girl's name is Anita, and she introduces me to her friend Susan, and for the first few weeks I join them for lunch. I see Gina, La Vecina's daughter, and her friend Rita when we walk around. They invite me to eat with them and I accept. Anita and Susan are cool with it.

Lately Gina has been missing a lot of school. Rita and I are becoming better friends, and I am more comfortable with school now. Not to worry, like my Dad always says.

Dad has started talking to us about the early days again. We have just eaten squash for dinner and Mom says, "My dad didn't have a chance to throw calabazas when Tom came to ask if I would marry him."

Dad breaks in with, "I was afraid to take my parents to ask for your mom's hand in marriage. I took my cousin Sylvestre instead. Of course, your mom said yes."

I laugh. "You say 'of course,' Dad, but what if she had said no? What then? I guess none of us would have been born, huh?"

My father looks over at Mom. He smiles and touches her hand. "I was so nervous. I knew she'd say yes, but I had to ask Papá Fidel and I rushed into it."

I chuckle. "You goof!"

"Yes, he is a goofball." Mom agrees.

Dad sweeps his hand in the air to dismiss our comments. "Eee!" my father says, crunching his facial muscles and keeping his teeth together in a tight smile. "Listen to this. We were all sitting at the table afterward. Mamá Ninfa fixed us some food to eat. Empapá Fidel asked Sylvestre, 'Do you think it feels good to give your daughter's hand in marriage? It doesn't feel so good. Wait until you have a daughter someday and you give her hand in marriage. I'm going to ask you how it feels.'"

Mom blows air out of her nose in a half silent giggle and half reprimand, "¡Pendejo! He didn't even ask me! He asked my daddy first. He didn't say he had come for that! He came every weekend to see me, but he didn't say what he was up to."

Mom and Dad look at each other, and she goes on: "The following weekend Mom and Dad took me to buy my wedding dress at Hinkle's in Albuquerque. Two weeks later we got married. It was a big wedding. Everybody came."

I interrupt to ask, "How did you do that so fast? There wasn't even time to send invitations."

Mom shakes her head in a matter-of-fact way. "Back then we didn't send wedding invitations. Everybody tells everybody, and they hear it at church, and so everyone comes."

She continues, "Then the Sunday right before the wedding, we went to a fiesta in Mora. They raffled a sack of flour and I won it. Everybody said it was rigged. We made a lot of bread for the wedding with that flour. Mom killed a lot of chickens. Tom brought meat from Schwartzman's, where he worked."

"Who cooked?" I ask.

"Everybody helped, especially Tía Tere. She always helped my mom a lot."

"What about the men? Did they help?" I ask.

"Down there where the road collects water, you know, it was muddy and my daddy, my brothers, and Tom put gravel on the road so cars could pass through to our wedding fiesta at the house."

Some of my parents' stories make me realize how different things were for them from how life is today. I protest, "They hardly knew Dad and they put him to work?"

"Hey, everybody works when there is a wedding. Besides, your grampa wanted to see what kind of man I was marrying. Was he a hard worker or what?"

I say to Mom, "I guess he passed the test."

Mom says, "Ah heck, they loved him right away. I think they loved him more than they loved me."

"Mom, can we look at your wedding pictures again?"

Mom gets up from the table. "Wait here," she says and walks to her bedroom, returning with a picture album. We look at several pictures of her in a wedding dress. In one she is standing alone, a satin circle spread before her, with a bunch of flowers lying on top.

Mom points to each person in a photo of young women standing next to her. "This is Corina, this is Beatrice, my cousin Flora, and my madrina."

"You are all so young and beautiful!" I exclaim. "That's Aunt Bea and Aunt Corine?" I look harder at the picture. Mom's hair is curled and long and her smile is very big. Dad's sisters are very pretty. "Wow, this is cool. Aunt Bea is so young, look at her."

"Yes," Mom says, "we were very young. I was nineteen when I married your dad."

"Who are they?" I ask, pointing at the photo she holds in her hand.

"That is Uncle Manny and Aunt Mary."

"No. It can't be. That is Aunt Mary? She doesn't even look like herself. She has black hair and is really sexy."

Mom laughs. "Yes, even Aunt Mary was young at one time." She folds up the picture album. "We dated only six times, your dad and I, and then got married. And," she emphasizes, "we were alone only two of those dates. We wrote letters to each other every day for six weeks."

"Qué romantic. Did Grama ever get hold of your letters?" I tease.

"I hid the letters in a very good place. Yes, I made sure of that."

"You hardly knew him. I am surprised they let you marry him," Dolores says.

"How did you know if you loved him?" I ask.

Mom looks at Dolores. "They knew Uncle Manny. They loved Uncle Manny and figured his brother was a good man too." Mom shrugs and blinks her eyes and says, "I guess they were right about that."

We all laugh.

Dad adds, pointing at Mom, "See there, that laugh is what I have always loved about your mama. Her laugh was the first thing that attracted me to her."

Mom smiles that great big smile she uses when she is happy, "Our wedding march started at the end of the driveway. Tío Alfonso played the violin.

Tom and I led the march. My tío danced and jumped around us as he played. He was funny. Everyone in the marcha clapped."

We are around the dinner table again, and Daddy is telling us a story about the move from Atrisco to Corrales. To me, it is a continuation of the story about their wedding.

Dad's face changes when he starts to tell a story. It is like he is a child watching an elephant at the circus. "There was a guy who put Manny wise to the taxes, you know, late taxes. Ooh, I don't remember his name now. He was a good guy and worked for the tax department in Bernalillo. Manny got information from him and we ended up with these eight acres here."

I thought all the property was my father's. "Uncle Manny owns some of this?"

"We bought two properties, one in Peralta and this one in Corrales. We each paid half of the back taxes. And it was implied that we would share produce and other goods. That way I'd take full ownership of the entire acreage in Corrales, and he would take Peralta. I did all the fencing and whatever. I planted and tended the farm."

"Is that why Aunt Mary comes here and takes sacks of chile and bushels of tomatoes and fruit?" I ask.

"You mind your own business," my father says, though his look alone was enough of a reprimand. I understand now why Aunt Mary has so much say-so around here.

"Anyway," my father says, clearing his throat roughly, indicating I am out of line, "this piece belonged to the Martinezes up in the *lomas*. We had to clear the land of cottonwood trees. I hired a guy to help me pull those out of here. It was bosque here."

It is true, though, that Aunt Mary bosses my mother around, and Mom just lets her. Mom and Dad are generous to everyone. People drop in while we are having lunch or supper and they are always invited to eat with us, even if what we cooked looks like only enough for the nine of us. Mom always says, "Never be stingy with food. There is always enough." She has a Spanish saying, *Para todos hay, comen no arrebaten.* She reprimands us if we try to grab extra food for ourselves. I am always surprised when we share with a whole other family and still have a tiny bit leftover. Mom is right.

When someone is bashful about joining us at the table, she says, "*Si deseas algo para comer y si no lo comes, a tu lengua le saldrá un grano.*" To desire this food and not eat it will cause a blister on the tongue. If they are still holding back or will not eat the last piece, she kids, "*Con vergüenza no llenas,*" meaning shyness will not sustain you.

I remember the time I was at Sally's house and how much we all laughed when Sally's father said, "*El hambre es cabrón,*" meaning hunger is a bitch.

Dad gives sacks of chile and vegetables and packages of meat to people all the time. He does not wait to be asked, he just gives.

"Papá helped me fence the property."

Dad's words pull me away from my thoughts and back to his story. He is talking about Grandpa Jesús.

"We had a good time together. Papá helped me a lot, especially when it was time to harvest the chile. I loved having him here with me."

I interrupt, "Grandpa Jesús was always so frail. I can't see him driving the tractor or anything like that."

"He wasn't always sick," Dad says, dragging out the word sick as if to say I have insulted his father. "He was strong and healthy just like me."

Dad always says, "Think before you speak." I need to remember that.

My father's tone softens and becomes playful when he recalls another incident. "One time when we were fencing, he buried his bottle of wine so that the wine would stay cool. He couldn't find it and accused me of drinking it or hiding it from him."

Dad is quiet for a moment. He reaches for a tortilla and spreads butter and a thin layer of jelly on it. He takes his time chewing a big bite, so I wait to hear what he will say next.

Dad does not disappoint me. "The opportunity was there, so we made the move to Corrales. It wasn't easy. We had a brand-new house in Atrisco."

Mom says, "I hated leaving my brand-new house and my neighbors. I liked living in Atrisco. The city bus stopped right in front of my house. I could go to work or to town so easily. I was not looking forward to living in the boonies."

Dad takes a sip of coffee and says, "We decided to come over here. It was February. It was a beautiful week, the first week. Ha ha. After that it got cold again.

"We brought Polidor's trailer and lived in that. At first we parked it way in the back, by the irrigation ditch. Your mama felt too isolated and was afraid, so we moved it right here. We lived in it for about a year, till I built those two rooms."

"Oh, I remember, Dad," I interject. "I remember coming to visit and there were only two rooms. One of them was the kitchen, right?"

Dad nods and continues, "Then we took the trailer back to Polidor. I don't know what he did with it. He sold it for literally nothing, but he had helped me out for a year. Then I worked on the rest of the house. I got materials to build this house from houses they were tearing down in Albuquerque, and from materials they threw away when they were building the houses in the Hoffmantown area. I patched pieces of drywall like puzzles to make the inside walls. The outside walls are all adobe."

Mom adds, "That part was really hard. Your dad and I would go for a ride and look at the brand-new houses in Hoffmantown. They were beautiful. Our house was coming along slowly. He worked hard every day, but things take time. I thought he would never finish it. And to top it off, strangers were living in my house in Atrisco. It was hard."

"They were not strangers," Dad says to Mom. "My cousin Ramon rented the house and he was a good renter."

I had been to visit Ramon at the house in Atrisco. I ask, "Did we have all those rose bushes growing along the fence and climbing up to the porch when we lived there?"

Mom says, "Oh, how I loved my roses. It was so hard to start my flower-beds all over again. It seemed all I had time to grow in Corrales were irises and hollyhocks. Every time I left for a visit to Mora, your dad would clean up the yard and make borders for larger flowerbeds, and he planted grass. I'd come home to my surprise and find what Tom had done and find everything so nice. Good memories."

I try to imagine us living in Atrisco, but I cannot remember anything about life there or anywhere before Mora. I was only a baby.

Dad returns to the story. "About that time, Clore Silva was the ditch rider in Corrales and he retired. Of course, Polidor was aware of that, and he contacted me and asked if I wanted to apply for the job. So I applied. Polidor had a lot of pull there. He had only been there a year or so, but the manager, old man Cole, had a lot of confidence in him. Several others applied from here, from Corrales, but I bid them all out, I guess. I got the job with Polidor's influence with management."

Mom interjects, "That is the good that came with the move. It was the perfect job for you. You could work on the house and keep a job at the same time. And even do the farming."

Dad smiles. "*Cuando una puerta se cierra, otras se abren.*" When one door closes and others open, we may lose something, but out of that more opportunities may come. He winks at Mom. "Right before our move to Corrales I bought a tractor and all the fittings for fourteen hundred dollars. I saved ten dollars every week in a jar I had buried until I had three hundred dollars. I used that three hundred dollars for the down payment. I had to make a payment once a year. That first year in Corrales I planted a lot of chile so I could sell it and make the payment. The chile was growing nicely. The plants were beautiful. Then a bad hailstorm wiped out the garden. There were no leaves left on the plants. It rained for days and the water saturated the ground and would not dry. It flooded badly. What do you do? It was so hard. We cried and we prayed."

Mom adds, "We would look out there at the fields and cry. We would walk outside and hug and cry some more. It was very hard. We kept telling each other that at least we had each other and our health. We had no money and it looked like we would not make any money from the chile either. We didn't have enough money to buy food. I was pregnant with Mark. Diana was a baby and Gloria, we had to send you away to live with my mom in Mora."

My mother clicks her tongue and continues, "At first we sent Tony, and after just about six weeks your daddy wanted to bring him back. We missed him very much. Then we both decided we couldn't send Dolores. She was our firstborn. So we sent you. Every day I cried for you. I'd be hanging diapers on the clothesline and just stand there with wet clothes in my hands and cry. Your daddy would find me looking out the window in the evenings, crying. I missed you. It was very hard to send you away."

Hearing Mom tell about me when I was a baby is strange. I don't remember too much about Mom or Dad until I came to live with them when I was six.

Dad interrupts my thoughts. "All our money down the drain, and all that work too. *Gracias a Dios*, the plants grew new leaves and we had green chile that year, but no red. There wasn't enough time for it to turn red before the freeze. I didn't make the money I'd hoped for. You never know what nature will bring. Somehow I managed to pay off that tractor."

I yearn for more explanations, more sorrow, more something about why I was sent away, but I don't ask. For an instant I feel a little tightening in the ridge of my nose and can feel my nose getting warm. I hold back tears and fear that if I speak, I'll cry.

Mom goes back to relating her memories. "Oh, sometimes we would run out of gas in the middle of making beans or on a very cold night. It was awful."

I can tell Mom really didn't like it in Corrales at first. "Why didn't you guys stay in Atrisco?"

"Your dad wanted to farm, and when he found this land, we just moved."

"What about Diana? When did she go to Atrisco to live with Grandma Patrocinia?" I ask.

Mom sighs and says, "Oh, that was another hard one. Diana was only eleven months old when she went there to live. My mother-in-law kept saying to me, 'You sent Gloria to your mother, why can't I have Diana?' I didn't know what to say. She would not let the subject drop. Finally I gave in and sent Diana to stay with them."

Not thinking, I say, "Wow, Mom. I guess you could have said no."

I say no all the time, I think to myself. In fact, I get in trouble for saying no or for speaking up for myself. I have no trouble using strong words in defense of my brothers and sisters. One evening at the dinner table I spoke up in defense of my father because Uncle Junior was insulting. Dad said to me, "Don't speak to your uncle in that tone. You hear?"

I was hurt by Dad's reprimand until he said to me later, away from the table, "Jita, your uncle is just young. He thinks he knows it all. I don't have to defend myself to him or anyone else. You don't worry about me. I can take care of myself if I have to. Okay? Understand? But you have to respect your elders. Always respect your elders."

I'm glad Dad confided in me like that. Dad is strong. Even when he acts weak, he is really being strong. I understand now and am proud that he didn't react to my uncle's remarks.

Mom has not gotten on me for my outburst. Maybe she wishes she could have said no to Grandma Patrocinia. I wonder, though, can Mom say no to anybody? I think not to her elders. She sure can say no to us kids.

Piñon for the Pickin'

"**R**ise and shine," Dad calls through the halls in his cheerful early morning voice full of vibrato and a New Mexican Spanish accent. In his army days he was summoned out of bed with those words, and now it is tradition at our house. Some mornings it is just fine, when we look forward to some exciting event like today, but other mornings the cheerful sound is plain annoying.

It is very early and Dolores struggles to awaken the baby. She tickles Edwina's nose, and then she removes the blanket and gently gives her a little shake before she lifts her into her arms.

Diana is awake and asking, "Do you see my shoes anywhere?"

Dolores is usually patient, but this morning she is in a hurry. "Where did you take them off?" she asks, and then says, "You're always barefooted. Check outside or in the TV room."

Dolores needs help. "Come on, Gloria, help me with Edwina. She needs a light jacket, and put her shoes on. Hurry, it's time for breakfast. I smell the bacon and Mom will want our help."

After breakfast we all climb into the green Chevy, Dad's new truck. Edwina and Joseph ride in the cab with Mom and Dad, and the rest of us sit in the truck bed. We stop in Alameda to pick up our friends, Charlotte and Sally. The drive to the Sandia Mountains will take an hour. Finding a spot to pick the piñon adds more time. My parents want to beat the heat.

The crisp chill this morning makes us gather closely under a blanket like newborn puppies keeping warm. The chatter and excitement build up. Riding along over bumpy dirt roads and smooth paved highways, we start to sing many of our favorite songs, "Oh My Darling Clementine," "The Ants Go Marching," "On Top of Old Smokey," "La Cucaracha," and "Allá en el Rancho Grande." We sing until the teasing begins.

"Move over, Rover," Tony says as he nudges Mark over the edge of the spare tire he is sitting on.

Shyly, aware that all eyes are on him, Mark repositions himself, saying quietly, "There is nowhere to move."

Tony continues with, "*Qué pasa*, how come you fell over, *ese?*"

Mark's eyes slowly rise to meet Tony's before he says, "You pushed me." I can tell he would like to say more but holds back.

Tony persists, "Was the truck moving too fast through that curve on the road for you, bro?"

I get a tight feeling in my chest watching Mark's discomfort, "Grow up, Tony!" I yell.

Turning a slight shade of red, Tony decides to quit. I think it is because Charlotte is with us.

The truck follows a dirt path that was once a road. Dad always likes hidden away places. We climb slowly upward. The small loose rocks make the truck slide from side to side. Suddenly all of us are sliding toward the rear of the truck. Tony and Mark slam into the tailgate. Tony and Diana laugh. For me it is scary, but I don't say anything. I am waiting for Mom to do something. She anxiously orders Dad to let her off.

"I can walk," I hear Mom say.

When he stops the truck, I quickly climb out. We walk side by side as we conquer the steep hill. The truck continues to fishtail before reaching the top of the hill where Dad waits for us to get back in the truck.

"You big chicken, you fraidycat, you're always afraid," Tony starts saying and Diana joins in. It is easy for me to choose teasing over a sliding truck.

"We're here!" Dad yells out as he stops the truck. We all jump out like kid goats. It feels so good to be in the mountains where the air is cool and fresh. The sun hits the ponderosa pines and a sweet warm fragrance like vanilla rises off of them. We grab our small tin buckets and each of us makes a run for the tree we think has the most fallen piñon. If Grampa had come with us, he would get up on the tree and shake it hard and nuts would fall right out of their cones, dropping onto a tarp beneath the tree. Plenty of full cones would add bulk to the harvest. The piñon would be sticky, but in minutes we'd have a whole lot of it. But Mom prefers we keep everyone's fingers away from the sticky sap.

Tony races from tree to tree, choosing carefully. "I've got the best tree on the whole mountain," he says. "Ándale, Mark! Let's show these girls how to pick piñon."

Mark is four years younger than Tony and considers his older brother to be the best at everything. No question about it. He goes along, happily.

Tony loves competition, so without responding to his comment, I take on the challenge.

Joseph wants to be with his brothers. "I'll help you too, Tony," he says and he begins to follow them. Mom calls Joseph back to her side, where Edwina will remain as well.

We divide into smaller groups, and as distance separates us, silence fills the large open space. The soft breeze and the sweet melody of a skylark remind me of the quiet peace I felt in the Mora Mountains and at my eighth-grade retreat. Chirping blue jays swiftly fly into view, parading their brilliant colors. I am free to feel God's presence.

Picking piñon is not a chore at the start of the day. We use our fingers like pinchers and gather nuts into our hands and toss them into metal buckets, making clanging rhythmic sounds. As the bucket fills, the sound changes to a quiet tapping. The ones with reddish-brown shells are good piñon. Some have a whitish-gray tint on a portion of the shell, which are *vano*. Without taking notice, I crack a vano in my mouth and quickly spit it out. The nut has withered away to dust that seems to explode in my mouth. I can't get rid of the horrible taste. I spit and spit to try to remove the rotten taste.

Sally and I work quickly and diligently at first. Tiny rocks dig into our knees right through the blanket we laid on the ground. The warmer it gets, the more clothing we remove. Moving from tree to tree, we work on filling our buckets. Repositioning our bodies is necessary; we move from squatting to sitting and stretching from side to side and back to our hands and knees. Slowly, not wanting to totally give up the competition, conversation starts taking priority over picking piñon.

I hear Mom's invitation to lunch. Hunger for her baked chicken and potato salad brings us together. My mouth waters at the thought of tearing into her delicious homemade bread. Gathering under a large shade tree, we empty our proud pickings into a *saco de harina* that holds twenty-five pounds. In the flour sack, the amount I picked seems like two handfuls. Without saying a word or showing interest, I watch as the others empty theirs. Tony has a full bucket already—how does he do it? Dad turns the truck radio on. The guys and Mom will not miss the World Series. We sit around, talking in hushed tones, eating and listening to the game. Tony works on getting a laugh. He pretends to walk like a very old man using a stick for a cane. He puts his lips over his teeth and pretends to gum his food, then begins talking in a weak, shaky voice.

The afternoon picking will not last long, as we tire of the task. The sun beats hot on our backs. Mom yells out so we can all hear, "Let's call it a day!" Happy to cooperate, we all run to the picnic spot and empty our buckets, ready to leave. Mom walks toward the truck and says, "Climb in, everybody."

It is hard to get all of us into the truck, but she eventually takes a final count. Dad drives slowly down the hill, only to find a locked gate at the opening. In the back of my mind I recall hearing a siren at least an hour ago. Now I am thinking that maybe it was a signal to leave or be locked in? I say nothing about it.

There is a feeling of panic as Dad orders us to get out of the truck and picks up a shovel. My brothers, using their hands and feet, begin to fill the arroyo with dirt, rocks, and branches. Dad says to Tony, "*Que andas hay con las manos peladas pendejo, levanta un garote hombre.*"

The air is tense as Tony obediently picks up a large stick to use as a tool to push dirt more efficiently than with bare hands. My father considers Tony a young man—no longer a child. They make a path just large enough to drive the truck out. I hear Mom whisper, "Gracias a Dios." I agree.

The drive back gets noisy again as we compare stories, and all the tension is left behind. We talk about things we saw or heard; who picked the most, ate the most, and naturally, who is the best. Then the other stories begin. We tell school stories, talk about boys we like, or girls we don't like. When my sisters and I don't want our brothers to understand, we sometimes use pig Latin. Our brothers just don't get it! Our pig Latin is not the one everyone else uses. We simply add ski to all the words. For example, I-ski Like-ski Robert-ski. We talk so fast; no one understands what we are saying.

Tony starts making up verses about two kids at our last school. They were not the most popular kids. "Roscina and Pati, sitting on a tree," he starts, and then adds his own phrases. He is merciless in his description of what they do: "Roscina and Pati, lying on a bed, Roscina farted and Pati fell dead."

Tony gets laughter, which only encourages him to get cruder. Rosina wears glasses that are too big. They slide off her nose, which makes her look like she has four eyes. She stutters in that squeaky, nasal voice.

Tony may tease her, but the girls in our class tend to exclude her. Pati may be from the wrong side of the tracks, but boys are more forgiving of differences, and he is never left out.

The wind generated by the speeding truck sweeps across our faces as our hair blows in all directions. We stand with plenty of space between us, holding on to the *barandales*. Barandales are used to keep a cow in transport in the truck or hold in bales of hay. They are made like jail bars, only they run horizontally, not up and down.

Tony and Diana begin to climb the barandales and we hear Mom yell to them, "Get down from there! You know it's dangerous." Naturally they try again and get the very same response: "Get down from there. Now, I say!"

Dad says the very same words as if they rehearsed them, only he adds, "*Animales*."

Dad drives our friends to their homes in Alameda. Home at last, we make a mad dash for the bathroom, where we form a long line. The boys are lucky—they go out back behind the haystack. My bladder nearly bursting, I secretly wish I could do that too.

Mama roasts piñon in the oven on a thin cookie sheet, and Dad roasts some in a large skillet on top of the stove. They are funny; they have a competition going about which way is faster and better. The piñon is stirred so it will cook evenly and not burn. A sweet nutty aroma fills the entire house, drawing us one by one to the kitchen table, where we wait in anticipation. We only have to wait about twenty minutes.

We've brought back enough piñon to snack on while we watch *Bonanza* or *The Ed Sullivan Show* on television all winter. Tomorrow we'll fill our pockets or pencil pouches and share with our friends at school. Dad will take some to Grandma Patrocinia and Aunt Bea.

Our bellies full, our day complete, we say our prayers and wish we did not have school tomorrow.

Dad's Hunting Surprise

Preparations for a hunt are as strategic as the hunt itself. Fig Newtons, potato chips, homemade tortillas, frijoles, chile, papitas, and plenty of eggs and bacon are packed side by side with the hunting rifles, sleeping bags, and flashlights. The camper is loaded with extra blankets, clothing, jackets, and gloves. Where will they find room to sleep? "Ándale, muchachos, let's get a move on!" I hear excitement in Dad's voice. Good-bye hugs, kisses, and good luck wishes are given hours before the sun comes over the mountain.

Departure at this hour is important in order to take advantage of a full day to track the deer. Never mind that Tony has not found gloves and Mark can't find his red cap. "Okay, boys, gotta have that red. Like I always say, red can't be mistaken for a deer, and hunters wear red for safety. Safety comes first." Aware of the lost gloves and cap, Dad adds, "You probably already put them in the truck last night when we packed."

Dad hunts in Lindreth and La Ventanita and will be gone four or five days. "Prim," my father's cousin Luvine Contreras, rides with Dad and my brothers. Accompanying them in their own trucks are Uncle Leonard and company, and Uncle Juan and sons.

Mom, my sisters, and I take on the chores of feeding pigs, chickens, horses, and even milking the cows while the men are gone. Hunting season gives us special time together. We cook as little and eat out as much as possible. Mom has her favorite places to eat: Polly's Kitchen for the best fried chicken and affordable prices; an Italian restaurant off Claremont between First and Third Street; China Town for Chinese; and sandwiches at home. We sometimes go to a movie theater to see movies instead of the drive-in. We have different kinds of fun while they are away.

As usual, when the hunters return, we run out to greet them. As predicted by Dad, they bring home a deer. Later he will cut the meat into steaks and roasts, which we'll wrap and freeze; some meat will be cut into thin slivers, spiced to taste, and dried for jerky. Everyone in the hunt will share the meat. For the moment, however, they have been missed. The reunion is cheerful until the stories begin.

We are all still standing outside next to the truck as Dad starts telling about his adventures over the past few hours. "We are heading home. Right below La Bajada I see a line of cars," Dad begins. He has that mischievous smile he wears when he knows there is going to be trouble. "Of course, it means a tag checkpoint. The warden flashes his light at me and says, 'Any luck?'

"I told Mark and Tony not to answer any questions. Let me do the talking, I said to them. I kept my voice calm, ha ha, and answered the warden: 'Yes, sir. One deer and a coyote.'"

Mom does not hesitate a second. "What are you talking about?"

Dad tries to laugh it off, saying, "I brought home a coyote."

Mom fails to see any humor in the situation. "¡Sanamagón! What were you thinking? You could have been put in jail."

"Hōney, hold on. You can see I'm not in jail."

"Don't hōney me, you crazy man. What happened?"

"The warden pointed the flashlight up over the truck, must've seen the deer tied up there. Then he walks to the rear and opens the camper door. I tried to distract him by asking, 'Officer, did you find the deer?' Then I had no choice but to tell him the coyote was in the camper shell behind the truck.

"The warden flashed the light in my face again and said, 'You can't take home a live coyote! What in the world do you intend to do with it?'

"I told him that I have a license to trap and plan to use the urine to camouflage the metal smell on my coyote traps."

Mom shakes her head and says, "I don't believe you. You could get your boys into trouble. You never think about that."

"No, no. I would never let that happen." Dad puts his arm around Mom's shoulders. "You know better than that."

Mom pulls away. "What happened next?"

"He confiscates the coyote and starts writing the ticket. It's a hefty fine. I told the boys to stay in the truck and went over to where the warden stood. I noticed a pile next to him on the ground. I say to him, 'Those are my traps, sir.' He says to me, 'I confiscated those from another vehicle.' I told him again, those are definitely my traps. I start explaining to him again that I have a license to trap. Then I took out my trapping license and showed it to him. And all he says is, 'You'll have to talk to the judge about that.'"

Mama starts into Dad again. "You know they have checkpoints, and you could have gone to jail. I can't believe the things you do! What are you going to do now, you sanamagón?"

Dad shrugs as if to say, who cares, and answers Mom. "My court date is on the ticket. We'll just have to wait and see what happens." His casual attitude and his use of the word *we* did not make her happy.

Weeks later we realize how Dad's luck follows him everywhere, even to his hearing.

The judge fines Dad for having a live animal in his vehicle, and once the judge validates ownership, Dad gets his traps back.

Las Fiestas

May brings the San Ysidro fiesta. I'm excited about the teenage dance at Perea Hall. The adult dance is being held at the new parish hall. I am asking permission to go to the teen dance when Dad starts telling us about the fiestas when he was young.

"Oh boy," Dad says. When I hear this I know he's had an enjoyable memory pop into his head. "We walked all over Albuquerque to get to every fiesta in town. Martineztown, Armijo, Alameda, Old Town—we went to them all. By golly, we even rode on horses to Mountainair. Later on, when we had an automobile, we'd drive to Santa Fe."

I'm surprised because Dad doesn't like to dance much. Mom gets him out there because she loves to dance, but he only dances as few as he can get away with.

"I remember," Dad is saying, "driving up La Bajada in those days was very steep and you climbed high to the top, and then down was just as bad. One time it snowed and we were going to the Santa Fe fiesta. The car started to heat up climbing the hill. We got snow and put it on the radiator to cool it off. We did that several times. Later on we learned to take water jugs."

People form lines for raffle tickets and to get into Perea Hall. I don't know half of these people. Many came from Bernalillo and Alameda. I squeeze my way through a group of guys at the front of the hall.

The room is lit by one bulb that hangs over the musicians. Benches line the walls and girls sit shoulder to shoulder. Some are standing by their boyfriends or other girls. I spot Rita and our friend Juliet and rush right over to them. "Hey guys, how's the band?"

Rita is the only one who can hear me over the music. "They play everything. Rancheras, cumbias, waltzes, polkas, country and western, and even rock. They're good."

"Seen any cute guys?"

"A few. Look over there." She points and then adds, "I like your dress. Is it new?"

"My aunt Mary bought it for me last summer. It's pretty, huh."

The band starts to play "Ojitos Verdes" and a guy in a cowboy hat and boots comes over to ask Rita to dance. Juliet is already out dancing, very close I might add, with George Gonzales. He is the best polka partner, but he does not even look my way. He is in love with Juliet. I'm wishing for a partner just so I don't stand here looking desperate.

Feet maneuver round and round on the pinewood floor. Finally, I dance a few rounds. Tony Martinez is a very good dancer, and I dance with him even if he was mean to my brother when we were in grade school. I am glad Rudy Lucero and Marty Perea like to dance with me. They like rock songs. Rudy and I dance like we are dancing around a bon fire like Indians dancing at a powwow. It is the latest, along with the slide, the jerk, the funky chicken, the funk, and just moving with the music. Mom and Dad actually let me come without them, so I am free to dance my heart away, to move to the groove.

A cute guy I have never seen in Corrales asks me to slow dance to an oldie by Ritchie Valens. He is about eight inches taller than me. He's slender, has black wavy hair, nice eyebrows, and straight teeth. I just ruined our first dance, though. I wanted to talk about something, anything. I said, regarding an older couple dancing close by, "Look at those two old fogies; they're all lovey-dovey. They should be at the other dance." I even made a face and rolled my eyes.

He looked down at me. His long lashes made his eyes look dreamy. I thought he might really like me. I scooted really close to this cute partner. Then he said, "Those are my parents."

I wanted to run and hide. I stuttered, making up some sort of conversation, only to make a bigger fool of myself. I guess the best way to learn a lesson is to feel the embarrassment. I will never poke fun at strangers again.

Ralph Rodriguez is very tall and has to bend to dance with me. I suppose we might even look silly, but I don't care. I have liked him for a long time.

Outdoor Mass on Sunday brings people from neighboring towns. Our procession leads us from the old church to the new. We sing "San Ysidro Labrador," stop to bless the ditch, and arrive at the hall for entertainment and food.

I walk around with friends, talking and flirting with guys. Every guy I see, even the ones I have known for years, has become more interesting and better looking for some reason. Fragrant blooms on fruit trees and heavily loaded snowball bushes add to this restless sensation inside me that makes me feel like singing, hugging, or kissing everyone I see. Even the older folks are in love. Dancing outside on the church grounds unites young and old.

Everyone in town is here, farmers and their wives and children. During fiesta time, first we pray, then we play.

4-H

My parents put us in 4-H. At my first meeting with parents and members I listened to the speaker tell a story about his adventure in the mountains. He had taken his kids to pick piñon. He said, "It was a sunny New Mexico fall day. We each had buckets and began to pick. My boys are eight and nine years old. They came to me with full buckets, and so quickly too. I was very impressed." The speaker laughed. "They said to me, 'I don't know why you like these. We don't like the taste at all.'" The speaker laughed again. When he laughed, I started to get the picture. The speaker continued, "I reached for a handful of piñon, thinking maybe they were eating bad nuts, only to discover they had picked rabbit droppings."

The whole gym full of people laughed. We signed up. Some of our friends from school were already members and some kids I knew from church were members too.

4-H these past years have taught my sister, Dolores, and I how to sew and embroider. Mrs. Carstens, our leader, has even given my mom tips on how to sew clothing for us.

In my first year of sewing Mrs. Carstens had us sew an apron and pillowcases. I embroidered the four-leaf clover in green to represent 4-H on the pillowcases. I received a white ribbon for that project at the county fair. I earned a green ribbon for my tortillas another year. Over the following years we learned how to sew blouses, skirts, dresses, and pants.

Tony was made famous in 4-H, at least to us. Mom has saved the article from the *Albuquerque Journal* that shows Tony at age ten bending to pose with his almost-year-old gilt. The Kiwanis club started a program implemented by the 4-H club. One young member was to raise a female piglet. When the sow gave birth, another young person was to keep the chain going by raising one of her piglets. For months, my brother made sure to feed his gilt ground corn supplemented with other grains and slop in order to fatten her up. On occasion Rex O'Keson, the 4-H leader of this program, saved table scraps to feed the piggy. Tony and his gilt won the blue ribbon. He looks proud and happy in the picture.

Tony also takes entomology with Mrs. Sally Jo Shaver. He goes around catching butterflies and bugs, then displays them in a glass case. Each insect has a typed label to identify it. He makes a very beautiful exhibit for the county fair. Sally Jo Shaver also leads 4-H tractor and farming.

Mrs. Miller, our baking and cooking leader, has assigned Dolores to demonstrate how to make tortillas. We are in the 4-H building on Indian School. Dolores sounds so professional. Each ingredient is premeasured and in little glass containers. She faces her audience and smiles and is using clear speech. She could be on a television cooking show.

In about an hour I get to demonstrate how to make a bed. I'll show how to tuck the sheets in the corners and pull the sheets tight. I hope I can look at my audience like Dolores is doing, but I already feel nervous about getting up on stage in front of everybody.

Advanced sewing groups had a fashion show and walked on stage in their dresses, coats, blouses, and pants. The clothes looked store-bought.

Mrs. Arandale teaches dog obedience. Her group will demonstrate what many dogs in Corrales have learned. It's too late for our dog, Tiger, but Tiger is perfect anyway.

Qué Bueno Que Se Acabo la Escuela

Yay, school is out! I have been offered a couple of jobs this summer. I wrote to Grama and she agrees it is good for me to work and make some money. Every time I have to make big decisions, I write to Grama. She helps me see reasons to choose one way or the other. I also write to Grama when I feel guilty about things, feel lonely, or unloved. Grama knows what to say. I love getting her letters.

I'll miss Grama and Grampa. Grama and I figured out that I can go to Mora for only two weeks before starting my new jobs. After I leave, Diana is planning to spend some time with Grama.

Ah, Mora is such a welcome change. The rain wets the ground and brings up the memories from years I have passed here with Grama and Grampa. I am so glad to be here.

Grampa and I went to the post office in Mora today. I stayed in the truck and later decided to get down and go inside. I was a ways from the door when Grampa came out. He was looking at the mail in his hands. A boy whistled at me as I walked toward Grampa. Grampa yelled at him, "*¡No es borrega!*" I was so embarrassed, I ran back to the truck.

Grampa said to me, "You have to demand respect from boys. If you let them treat you like nothing but sheep that they whistle at, that is how rude they will always treat you. Do you understand?"

I listened and loved him for loving me enough to teach this lesson. He and Dad preach the same message when it comes to boys.

I have hitched a ride with Uncle Manny and Aunt Mary and am on my way to Corrales. It was so hard to say good-bye to Grama and Grampa. I wanted to stay, but I have bills to pay now. Grama and I cried like usual when we said good-bye. My sister, Diana, will ride back with Uncle Manny to Mora when he returns. That should be good for her. I know Grama and Grampa will like it.

Babysitting for the neighbors on weekend nights buys me records, mascara, and other things I like. Cleaning house for Nena is how I pay for my braces. I pay $26 a month. Mom paid the down payment of $104. I paid my dentist from my savings; the bill was $86 for the x-rays, cleaning, and all my fillings. Dad says, "Save some of your money, jita. Open an account at the bank and save." Now I see why.

Dolores has offered me her Sunday school babysitting job at the Presbyterian church in Alameda. I can go to Mass early and walk to Mrs. Akerman's house, and she will drive me to her church. I'll work from ten to twelve and earn more money in two hours than I earn in a full day of cleaning house.

Some weekends I spend with Sally. We walk to the soda fountain at Yonomoto's little store and sit in the Japanese garden with a soda or ice cream, telling our deepest secrets. Or we walk the ditchbanks of Corrales, listening to the transistor radio and singing. On Sundays we go to Mass at San Ysidro Church or Nativity in Alameda. We talk on the phone almost every night.

The Adobe Theater job, serving refreshments between acts, is going to be more fun than work. I can attend the plays for free. I like the atmosphere. People dress up, there is loud chatter, and everyone is excited to have refreshments under the summer stars. I like watching the way people act and how they talk to each other, and I am not referring to the actors. Summer nights are fresh but not cold, and I love being outdoors. We serve lemonade, tea, and punch. Dolores and I work together. Watching the plays is a bonus.

Grandma Patrocinia has invited me to stay a few days with her. She likes to brush and braid my hair. I am too old for that, but I kneel in front of her anyway. I like the way it feels. Every night we pray the rosary. Actually we pray three. She says that we are really supposed to say fifteen decades. We pray in Spanish on our knees the whole time. For the very last rosary, we say the short version, replacing every decade of Hail Marys with Grandma Patrocinia saying, "*Jesús mío perdón y misericordia por los méritos de vuestras sagradas llagas.*" And we respond, "*Eterno Padre yo te ofrezco las sagradas llagas de nuestro Señor Jesús Cristo para curar las llagas de nuestras almas.*" In place of reciting the Lord's Prayer, Grandma Patrocinia says, "*Eterno Padre te ofrecemos nuestras almas.*" We respond, "*Has que me alma no se pierda ni muera sin confesión, Amen.*"

After we finish our rosaries I get ready for bed. Grandma Patrocinia goes into the kitchen. I walk in to say good night. She has been reading the Bible like she does every night. She is sitting with her head bent and eyes closed. For a moment I think she has fallen asleep. She looks up and summons me for a kiss and a blessing on my forehead.

Crazy Cow Stories

I am finding that there is never a dull moment on the farm. For three years from April to October my father, along with Max Perea, Apolinario Montaño, and Clore Silva, all Corrales residents, took advantage of the government allowing the use of the bosque for grazing cows. Dad means to call these men in hopes they can shed light on our cows' current disappearing act.

The cows are lost in the bosque. Our entire family is in the bosque gathered around Dad, listening to his instructions: "We'll divide into two groups, one going south, the other north." He is so serious. He keeps talking as he divides us up. "Look for fresh tracks and follow them. Listen for the cowbell. When you hear the bell, follow the sound. The lead cow will lead you to the others or they will be close by. We are not playing here, so don't be messing around. You won't hear the bell if you are making noise." Dad groups me with Mom, Mark, Diana, and Edwina. He continues, "When you find them, bring them back to this corral. We will all meet here with or without the cows. Don't leave until we have all returned to this spot. Do you understand?"

It is getting hot and Mark, Diana, and I have walked south for miles and not seen a cow. Edwina wanted to be carried and tired Mom out, so they stayed behind to rest. Where could fifteen cows disappear? And that is if they are all together. Dad said sometimes they split up. Those cows must have gone in the other direction. Maybe they even left the bosque.

My group of five is back at the corral where Dad told us to meet. Mark and I stroll over to the shade of a cottonwood and sit. "Interesting corral. How did you guys make it?" I ask.

Mark is only twelve but has been of tremendous help to Tony and Dad for a few years. He proudly explains, "We tied salt cedar branches to the flood control jetty, the cable, and made this coyote fence. It's not the best corral, but it works. Usually it works, anyway. We lock up the lead cow; whatever works to keep them in the area."

"How the heck do they get lost? I thought they used a trail and could find their way back. You know, follow the leader."

"You're right, cows use the trail to get to water or return to the corral. They browse for food here and there and know their way back, but you know, grass is greener on the other side. They like to eat and go off on their own. Sometimes one or two of the cows get ornery and will not follow the leader and they get lost."

The shade sure feels good after that long walk. Fanning my face with my hand, I turn to face Mark. "Why is Dad keeping them here anyway?"

"It allows the alfalfa pasture to grow so we'll have winter food for the cows and the horses."

"You know, Mark, it's kinda cool to be helping you today. I'd'a never walked all the way to the bridge on my own."

"Yeah, I usually like it here. I have to come really early in the morning to milk the cow. It is a new experience every day. Things happen, you know. If we keep the calf in the corral, the mama cow stands guard and keeps close. Sometimes we put the mama cow in the corral and that keeps the calf around. But no matter how careful we are, either the calf gets to the mama or the cow or calf can get out of the corral, and then I get in trouble two ways."

"Why's that?"

"Well, for the milk, *tú sabes*. The calf drinks the mama dry. And then sometimes on the way home I fool around and trip or knock the bucket of milk over. That's bad too. Dad and Mom get mad at me when that happens, depending mostly on how bad we need the milk. Crossing the log over the clear ditch is a balancing act. And riding the bike sure isn't a good idea; the levy is sandy and too often I swerve and lose control."

"You're funny. There has to be an easier way to get milk and stay out of trouble."

"Once in a while Dad lets me drive as far as the ditch and back. Those are the easiest times."

Dad and Tony join us at the corral. "Any luck?" Dad asks. Their group showed up empty-handed too.

Tony declares, "Polly and Daisy both wear a bell around their stupid necks. We didn't hear a single bell out there. Boy, it's hot! And that Molly takes off every chance she gets. She's the bad influence."

"There's a Dolly too, right?" I ask.

"The whiteface jersey." He rolls his eyes and answers me like I'm stupid. "Dolly and Polly, the Guernsey, provide the family with most of the milk, you know."

I make a comment just for the sake of conversation. "I remember when Dolly and Polly were calves and we fed them milk in buckets with large *tetas.*" We would make powdered milk and feed the calves from buckets with long artificial nipples attached. "I didn't know they were already cows giving us milk."

"You're right, you don't know anything about anything," Tony says. Sometimes I just have to ignore Tony's remarks or I would punch him and get myself into trouble with Mom.

Dad turns to Mark, "Did you see any signs of the cows? How far did you go?"

Mark answers quickly, "We first looked at the *isla* by Rutherford's, but they weren't on that island, so we walked all the way to the Rio Grande Bridge. Still no sign."

Tony wipes the back of his neck and says, "Them damn cows are usually over there by the Prices'. Sometimes they roam farther north to where we dam the water in Bernalillo to direct it to Corrales. Today they are hiding out but good."

Mom and Edwina walk over to where we are. Dad rests his arm over Mom's shoulder and says, "Let's go on home, have some lunch, and make some calls. Maybe someone has seen them."

After lunch Tony mounts his horse Blackie and Mark rides Frisky to the bosque. They check the corral first, then ride across the river to the Sandia Pueblo reservation. Our cows are grazing without a care in the world. My brothers round them up and bring them back to the west side of the river.

Tony and Mark come in the door with smiles on their faces. But they can't tell Dad that they found our cows because he had to go check on a call about a break in the ditch.

During dinner we listen to Tony and Mark retell their victory story. Dad is back and all nine of us sit around the table enjoying Jell-O and fruit.

Then Tony, the greatest storyteller, starts telling us about past cow experiences. "One time the bull was lost at the reservation for three whole weeks. He was having fun with all the Indian cows, ha ha."

Tony makes me laugh.

"Domingo offered to keep the bull on his property until the end of the season and then would bring him back to the corral, but instead you went to get the bull. Do you remember, Dad?" He doesn't wait for an answer. "You rounded him up and took him straight to the sales ring in the South Valley and sold it at the auction."

Mom interjects, "Do you remember what happened on the way to the auction?"

"Whatever happened, that bull deserved it," Tony answers.

Mama shakes her head. "Anyway, Eloy went with your dad to take the bull. They were at the stoplight on Coors and Central. The bull forced the gate of the barandales open, jumped out of the truck, and ran away as fast as he could. They had the hardest time getting him back in the truck."

"Damn bull!" Tony remembers. "I am so glad we finally are rid of him. He was nothing but trouble."

Everybody wants a chance to talk about the cows. One story leads to another and Mom can't wait to tell hers. Mom begins with this remark: "I have lots of crazy cow stories if you want cow stories." She has our attention. Dad smiles with interest. Tony sits there with his hands folded in front of him, legs stretched out under the table, acting like he's heard it all before. But arched eyebrows and a slight curve of his lips give away the fact that he is anxious to hear what she has to say.

Mom waves her hand in front of herself as though she is shooing away a fly, but what she wants is to hush us up. "I tied the cow to the tree to graze on the front lawn. She got all tangled up from going around the tree so many times and the noose tightened around her neck."

I remember how worried we were about that cow.

Mom is frowning. "We tried to let her free, but it was too tight and she kept struggling and struggling trying to get free. Then she fell and hit her head and one of her horns broke off."

Dad and Tony stare in disbelief because this is the first they have heard about this.

"Yes," Mom continues, "she was bleeding and she passed out. I sent Viola to get the vecino. I planned to have him help me slit her neck and drain her blood so we could save the meat. But when the vecino came, he cut the rope instead, and she regained consciousness. She was still bleeding so I taped a Kotex where her horn broke."

We all laughed, remembering the running around here and there, trying to free her, desperately trying to save the poor cow.

"Where was I?" Tony asked. He was usually the one to take care of things whenever Dad was not around.

"All of you boys had gone fishing with your dad. I was not going to admit that I was ready to kill her, so I never told your dad that part of the story."

Dad smiles and says, "Don Juan told me the whole story anyway. You can't keep any secrets from me."

Mark and Joseph leave the table to go outside, and Diana takes Edwina to the other room. The rest of us sit ready to hear or tell more stories.

Tony sits quietly, holding his head between two fists. Suddenly he bursts out, "Damn!" By the gravity in his voice I can tell he is about to say something serious.

"That river can be dangerous. Looks dry—so I start to cross over. My horse already knows we are going to the other side. Suddenly, Blackie sinks into the quicksand, nearly throwing me off. It's happened to the cows too; they are sucked down all the way up to their bellies."

I can't understand why Tony took the risk. "Can't you tell before crossing that it's quicksand?"

Tony sighs and his eyes roll up and around before holding me in an offended gaze. I could just punch him, and I would if I thought Mom wouldn't beat me after. I wish he didn't treat me like a bother. Tony thinks he knows everything. He continues to look and talk directly at me. "It looks a little muddy, but it is a dry muddy. It's hard to tell. Anyway, we have to drag them out with a rope, pull on their tails, or push them from behind. It's scary. We don't want to lose them."

Suddenly it occurs to me how important Tony's help is to Dad. Tony is very responsible. He really cares. My thought is interrupted by the start of another story.

This time Tony's voice has a touch of humor. "One hot day, my friend Nappy hit a cow with a rock to guide her in the right direction and knocked her out. Dad, you would have killed me if you had known. We were so worried, we waited a while before coming home."

I look at Dad and he is nodding his head. "Ah ha. And?"

"We were thinking up stories to tell you, you know, to explain why the cow was dead and how it happened. We all sat on the hot sand not wanting to come home. But about half an hour later, she woke up on her own, and in a daze she walked back to the corral. We were so relieved."

Dad shakes his head. "That's *one* story you are telling me. I was a kid once—I'm concerned about the ones you aren't telling me."

Thinking about saving a cow's life, I address Mom. "Didn't you save a bloated cow once?"

"Oh yes," Mom says, with a little laugh. "That was Mitsy. She ate too much wet alfalfa and she got bloated. I had to stab the side of her stomach and put a hose down her throat in order to save her. She belched and let out some gas—it blew out like wind. The smell that came out of her was horrible." Mom wrinkles her nose as if the smell was present as she spoke.

"What would've happened if you hadn't stabbed Mitsy?"

"They can get really sick and then die," Dad and Mom answer in unison.

Mom finishes with, "You have to let the gas out. I hated when things like that happened and your dad wasn't around."

Dad scoots his chair back. "Okay, I'm ready for some TV. Coming?" Only my mom follows him to watch television.

Near the end of summer four of our cows found their way out of the bosque and over to "dead man's curve" at the south end of Corrales. A delightful amount of hay sat at the Justice Feed Store. Frothy mouths moving from side to side gave evidence of their guilt. Eyes hidden by long curly lashes blinked with joy. Knowing nothing about what is mine and what is yours, they continued to feast.

Robert Swallows, the owner, had the cows impounded and Dad had to pay a penalty fee before he could get them back, and he also had to pay Robert Swallows $150.

The talk around the dinner table that evening and for a good week was lively. Tony stated, "I doubt they ate more than five bales. That guy is just a jerk. He could have called Dad and we would have gone for them and paid for the damage." Tony echoed my Dad's sentiments exactly.

And this was the end of bosque grazing for our cows. They left their mark along the Rio Grande. Fertilized the grass before living "happily ever after," with not a care in the world, back in our own alfalfa fields.

Not all the cows live happily ever after. The fate of a calf is to meet a hot iron and be branded for recognition. Recognition that this animal belongs to

Tomas Tafoya. Not wanting any full-blown bulls, a male calf will be castrated on his first birthday so that the meat will be tender and sweet. A female calf, later known as heifer, could also be butchered for man's consumption.

So it is that our freezer remains full of steaks, roasts, ribs, ground beef, and other various cuts of meat. Casserole was not in our vocabulary until Mom decided we needed variety. Dad refuses to eat casseroles and fries himself an egg instead. He insists, "I eat steaks and potatoes or frijoles and chile. Don't get fancy on me with pasta this and pasta that."

Butchering is a weeklong affair. Dad weighs the cow just to know the weight. Usually the weight is important when he plans to sell. Then as early as the sun rises, he kills the heifer, hangs its head down, drains the blood, removes the intestines, stomach, and organs, and then skins it.

Mom boils water and soaks the stomach in it, then empties the water and boils it again. With a sharp knife she scrapes the waffle side of the stomach until it is clean and white. The smell is horrendous. Mom has us help her wash out the tripe that lies in a large cajete. A galvanized tub is the only container large enough to hold the insides of a cow. We fill it with water. Mom squeezes out the green smelly contents from within the tripe onto the ground. We fill the tripe with water from the hose and rinse and rinse until the water comes out clear. The large intestine is saved to make *morcilla*, blood sausage, which is spiced with onion, chile seeds, garlic, and salt, and then put into the big intestine and baked and then sliced like meatloaf. More blood is used to make a blood pudding with sugar, applesauce, raisins, and cinnamon.

The heart, liver, and onions are fried in an iron skillet. We eat our treats with tortillas, fried potatoes, and red chile. The small intestines are boiled along with pieces of stomach to make *menudo*, a special soup served within days after butchering a cow.

Dad cuts the cow in quarters and hangs it in the walk-in cooler to age a few days. He says aging gives the meat a better taste. Dad will grind meat for hamburgers and meat loaf. The rest of the family will help wrap and label the special cuts of beef. He always puts some aside to give to Grandma Patrocinia and Grandpa Jesús and to his sisters and even to the neighbors. The rest will fill the freezer once again.

Crumbling Ground

Grampa often says, "We were born on the same day, married on the same day, and we will die on the same day." He is talking about himself and Grama. They share a birthday, April twenty-third. He is one year older.

It is five o'clock in the morning and the phone is ringing. Mom jumps out of bed, her heart thumping. No one calls at this hour unless there is an emergency of some sort.

Grampa cries at the other end of the receiver, "Nene, mi hija, your mama has died."

Mom screams, "No, Daddy, no!" They cry together for a while.

Grampa says, "Hurry and come. We will not call anybody until you get here."

"What happened to Mama, Daddy? How did it happen?"

"About four o'clock she started breathing different. She gasped for air. I shook her and tried to wake her but it didn't help. It was like she didn't even know I was there. I ran to Eloy's. It didn't take long. We ran back, but it was too late. She had stopped breathing. Ay, mi jita, ay, Dios mío!"

We all hear Mom's cry and come to her side. She signals for us to be quiet and holds her head with her free hand. "Daddy, we'll be there as soon as we can. Have you called anybody else?"

"No, you are the first one I called. Eloy brought me to Mora to use the phone."

Dad massages Mom's back as she relates the news. We stand there waiting for some clue as to what to do next and follow Dad's example, giving her a hug.

Mom wipes her eyes with her nightgown and looks at all of us. "We need to hurry. Pack enough clothes for a few days. We are going to Mora. Ándale!"

I pull out three pairs of pants and fold and pack them into the suitcase

I share with Dolores, Diana, and Edwina. I add three blouses. "I can't stand this. It takes too long to pack. Poor Grampa."

Dolores turns around and puts her arms around me. "I know. They are always together. It will be hard for him."

"Is this alright? You know, for the funeral?" I show her the navy blue dress. "Grama said I looked pretty in it." I chuckle. "You know what she said? She said, 'You can wear dresses that show your knees. You have pretty knees.'" My voice cracks when I say, "Nothing biased about Grama."

Dolores looks past me into the closet. "It really doesn't matter what you wear, but that is perfect. Take it."

Dad drives as fast as he dares. At the south end of Santa Fe Mom asks him to take her to Viola's house on Airport Road. "I didn't want to tell her about Mama on the phone," Mom explains. "She is pregnant and I don't want anything to go wrong. She might lose her baby or something." Losing her firstborn had left an invisible scar that Mom was not conscious of. Mom has informed her brothers Benny, Casey, and Fidel Jr. on the phone, but she takes precautions with her sister.

Faustín, Viola's husband, answers Dad's knock in pajamas. Dad doesn't go inside. He tells Faustín that we are on our way to Mora and why. Faustín then leads Mom and us girls into the bedroom and hugs Viola. Viola knows something is wrong the moment she sees Mom.

Mom sits on Viola's bed and hugs her. After telling her the sad news, she offers to help Viola pack. Viola asks to be alone and to go on ahead. "Really, I'll be okay. We'll be along soon."

It's eight o'clock and we are already in Las Aguitas. Uncle Eloy and his wife, Helen, open the door. Grampa is not alone. Mom and Grampa hug tightly, and without letting go, she reaches for Eloy. All three stand in a huddle, crying. Dad and the rest of us give hugs and kisses when they are freed from Mom's grip. Everything feels odd. I want to see Grama at the door the way she always waits for us, and I want to feel her hugs and kisses. Mom finally says, "*Vamos a ver la*, Daddy."

Grama lies on her bed under the quilt, her hands resting on her chest and her eyes closed. She looks as though she is sleeping peacefully, her gray hair mussed like any other morning. She has a slight smile on her mouth, as if dreaming a good dream.

Mom hugs her mother. When she moves away I climb the bed and lay across Grama's chest. I kiss her on the forehead and then her cheek. I touch her lips with my fingers. Mom gently pulls me away. "That's enough, mija."

Everyone else takes turns giving Grama a greeting of some sort: a nod, a touch of the hand, a hug, whatever, then they go to the kitchen when Eloy invites us to eat. "Helen is frying eggs. Let's go have breakfast."

I do not follow the others into the kitchen. Grampa and Mom remain to keep vigil. I ask, "Mom, is it okay if I comb Grama's hair?" Both she and Grampa say it is alright.

Grama's brush and gray hairpins are on her dresser. I have watched her comb her hair so many times, I can even imagine her sitting on the bench with brush in hand right now. "Is it okay if I wet her hair?" I am really afraid that I might pull out bunches of her hair. I do not know it is okay to comb a dead person's head.

Mom shrugs. "Go ahead. I'm glad you thought of combing her."

I sit at the head of the bed and spread my legs on either side of Grama. Her head rests on my lap as I brush the silver hair gently. "I want her to look like herself."

Grama's hair had a natural wave that curved softly around her face from a loose bun that she twisted in a roll and pinned in the back of her head. On special occasions she wore puffier hair arranged elegantly. I try to puff her hair but I have no luck making it look good, so I make a tight bun. It isn't perfect, but it looks combed.

The velorio is held the following night in Grama's house. She is placed in her coffin by the east window in the back bedroom. Relatives, neighbors, friends, acquaintances, and the religious come into the room from the middle bedroom and pass in front of the open coffin to pay last respects and walk out the door to the yard. Relatives lead in praying the rosary throughout the night, while others join in. Hymns saturate the souls of the living and the soul of the dead. *Alabados* and chants flow through the rooms, honoring the God that gives us life and takes it away. Hearts burn with spiritual connection to our beloved, my dead Grama. Her body, never to be left alone, is held in vigil throughout the night.

People keep coming in the door and bringing food. Coffee brews all night. Stories about Grama are told. Some are funny and make us laugh and some are more serious.

Ernest, her nephew, speaks of her with gratitude, "Tía Ninfa was always generous. We dropped by on Sundays with my brood, and she was always so happy to see us. She would say, 'Help me catch a chicken.' She chased them chickens and would catch one by the wing. She could catch them before anybody else. She chopped that chicken's neck with the ax and the chicken would run around chasing the kids." His laugh makes others in the room laugh. "In an hour or so we were sitting at the table, eating delicious fried chicken. No one could make fried chicken like Tía Ninfa. Nobody."

Rita agrees with her brother. "I loved coming to Tía's house. We always had fun here. We would go on picnics. We played games. She didn't believe in just work, work, and more work. I remember they took us to the movies to see *El Derecho de Nacer*. We always listened to the story on the radio when we came here to sleep. Tío Fidel liked that story."

Terry, Rita's sister, asks, "Is that the movie about a Negro woman giving birth to a white baby?"

Rita nods. "We would never have gone to the movies if adults didn't take us, and my tía and tío would take us."

I like what people are saying about Grama. Off and on I hear cries and laughter and prayer all mixed together. Grampa walks around and around as though in search of something.

The funeral Mass is over and cars drive in procession to the camposanto. The distance to the graveyard is too short. I know the last farewell is coming. I ride with Grampa to the cemetery. We both cry on the way there. Eloy drives and Mom sits in the front seat with him and Viola. The hearse leads the procession. Dad and the rest of our family follows someplace behind.

Father McHugh recites prayers, says a few words, and then everyone recites the Lord's Prayer together. People line up to give condolences one last time. Grampa, Mom, my uncles, and aunts walk to the coffin. It is lowered into the pit slowly. They each throw dirt over the casket as it descends. Somber faces look toward the pit while the rest of the extended family and friends also throw handfuls of dirt onto the coffin. We watch as nephews and sons shovel dirt over the coffin until a mound protrudes out of the ground. Grama's spirit left her body days ago and has gone home to Jesus. Our only comfort is in knowing that one day we will all meet again.

Louie Garcia, the funeral director from Las Vegas, came as a personal favor to Cleo, Grama's niece. He walks to Cleo with hands behind his back saying, "We have to go now." Cleo thanks him for everything and he drives away in the hearse.

Two days later I heard from my mother why Grampa was so burdened. What she told me made me sad because I thought Mom was going to cry, and there was nothing I could to do help her or Grampa.

Grampa had been unable to find Grama's wedding ring and wanted to have her buried with it. The night that she died, her fingers were swollen and the ring hurt her. She asked permission to remove it. Grampa saw Grama take the hanky from her dress sleeve and tie a knot around the ring. She was worried it might get lost.

Grampa had looked everywhere in the trastero, on the *cómoda*, kitchen windowsill, everywhere he could think of and could not find her ring. He had opened dresser drawers and boxes and looked under doilies and still no ring.

Mom cried, "My poor daddy! He said that she never took that ring off, not even once in their forty-two years of marriage." She sighed. "I helped him look for the ring too, but we just couldn't find it."

Mom said that in the morning before leaving for the funeral Mass, she swept the house hoping to find the ring in the *basura*. She finally had to say to him, "I guess this is the way it's supposed to be, Daddy. We'll have to bury her without her wedding ring."

The morning after the funeral, during breakfast, I heard Grampa ask Mom about Grama's belongings. "I don't want to rush you, but what should we do with your mama's things? You'll be going home and I cannot imagine what to do with all this."

I felt sorry for Grampa.

Mom answered, "We can divide her things between all of us. You keep what you want, and the rest of us will talk about what we want."

After lunch Casey, Junior, Eloy, Benny, Viola, and Mom discussed Grampa's request. Always interested, I hung around and listened.

Viola, not ready to think about dividing things, said, "All I want is Mom's saltshaker. The tin saltshaker that she uses for cooking."

Mom separated doilies and pillowcases that Grama had crocheted. "I'm making you a pile of these pretty things," she said to Viola.

Viola shook her head. "I don't want anything. Just the saltshaker is all."

Mom moved over to the bed where her parents always slept. She picked up the Santo Niño from the *nicho*. "Can I have the Santo Niño, Daddy?"

Grampa didn't answer right away. It looked like he was thinking about it. "That was one of your mama's favorite *santos*."

Mom saw a hanky laying in the nicho. Sure it was the hanky Grampa had described, she picked it up. "Look what I found. Her ring is right here."

Grampa hurried into Mom's view and put a finger to his lips. "Shh," he said, "you hold on to that."

Mom put it into her pocket. Later when she and Grampa were alone, he asked her, "Is it okay to give the ring to Gloria?" Mom told him I would be the perfect person to give it to.

Mom waited to give me the ring until we were on our way back to Corrales. She said, "Grampa wanted you to have this." I held the hanky and Grama's ring in my palms and smelled them. I kept smelling the hanky and looking at the ring. What a privilege to own Grama's wedding band.

This is how I came to hear the story about the precious ring I held in my hand.

When we drove up to our house after returning from Mora, the carport was full of sacks from one end to the other. We couldn't park the car in its usual place. Grama died on October sixth, and we left in such a hurry, not even concerning ourselves with the harvest. Don Juan picked our chile for us before the freeze would take it all. Mom started crying. "We have such good neighbors. They are more like family. *Mira*, honey, La Vecina and don Juan picked our chile."

For two days now we have not attended school. Mom says that it is hard to concentrate when we are in mourning. She cries all the time. I can see why she can't think. In fact, when I see her cry, I cry too. It is hard to believe that Grama died and that I will never see her again.

We have been separating green chile from red and make piles of red and piles of green and piles of *pintao*. The red for ristras and to dry, the green to roast and freeze or dry, and some to sell. The chile that is in between red and green, we call pintao, and it will be covered up with a tarp out of the sun until it is totally red. There is more red chile than green right now.

Grandma Patrocinia will come like she always does and take red chile home to make ristras. She makes the double-long six-footers and hangs them to dry all around the house. A passerby knows to stop if he wants to buy chile; no sign is needed. Dad has us help him tie three red chiles in a certain type of knot and make long strings of chile. He wraps the long strings around a long thick wire to make the ristra, which he hangs by the rafters on the roof. We sell our ristras too, and we do have a sign at the turn-off to our road.

Mom roasts bushel after bushel of green chile. When we get home from school, we peel and peel some more. Mom takes the peeled green chile and ties it on a string that she hangs out to dry on the clothesline. We put the rest in the freezer. It has turned into a tradition to peel our chile in front of the television while we watch the Miss America beauty pageant. We rate the contestants and choose the one we all think will win. This makes the work pass faster.

One thing I have learned is that every day may seem to be the same—change happens when we are not looking, whether we like it or not. People come into and go out of our lives. I want to hold on to the people, I want to hold on to the way things are and hope that they will always be, but I can't.

Mom cries all the time. She is always thinking about Grama, even while handling the chile. *Se enchilo los ojos.* Our hands don't burn from working with chile until much later, and they will burn for hours. But if we rub our eyes at any time while working with chile, our eyes will burn. That is what Mom teaches us over and over. Lately Mom's eyes are so red not only from crying, but from wiping the tears away with *manos enchiladas.* Poor Mom.

The days are unbearable for Grampa. He floats between Alamogordo, Corrales, and Mora. Week to week he goes to this son's house or that son's house and from Mom's back to his own house, only to return the following week. He walks the familiar path over the ranch and tries to feel at home, but what made him happy in this world is no longer of this world.

One evening, Eloy called my Mom and said, "Dad's leg is hurting and he is having trouble walking."

Mom said, "Have him come back and I'll take him to the veterans' hospital so they can check him out."

On December 12, 1967, doctors discovered a blood clot in the left leg. They say it will be fine with medication. He is allowed to walk, but only around the house. They will wait until after Christmas for any surgical procedures. They recommend he stay close.

I awake to sniffles in the night. The clock shows 2 a.m. I climb out of bed and go to the room where he is sleeping. "Grampa, I heard you crying." He sits up and in the darkness I see he wears those full-bodied long johns. I can see him wiping his eyes. "Do you want me to stay in here with you?"

"I am alright. You go on to bed, mi hijita."

"I miss her too." Without asking permission, I sit on the bed. I hug Grampa. His head bends forward and he cries into his hands. I look at the way his body hiccups with emotion. I hold back my tears and guide him back into the blankets. "I don't care what you say, Grampa, I am lying here with you." He turns his back to me and faces the wall. I hug him until he falls asleep. When I wake at dawn, I am still hugging him. I get out of bed as quietly as possible and go back to my room.

On December twenty-first, Grampa checks into the veterans' hospital. His pain has become worse. They put him on total bed rest and give him medication for his blood clot. Again surgery is postponed until after Christmas.

Mom and Dad go to the hospital to see Grampa every day. On December twenty-third, they bring us all to see Grampa. He jokes like always and it doesn't seem like he is sick. They allow only the kids who are fifteen and over into the hospital rooms. The rest of the family plays outside in the grass.

When Mom decides it is time to leave, I hate to leave him in the hospital. It feels like we are abandoning him. I give Grampa a hug and a kiss. I hold his hand. "Grampa, let us take you home and we can bring you back after Christmas. Anyway, they won't do surgery until after Christmas."

Grampa looks at me straight in the eyes. "*Tú sabes donde quiero estar, y con quien, para la Navidad.*"

I have no way to respond. I want to beg. My heart begs silently: "No, Grampa, you cannot leave us to be with Grama. You must stay with me. Please, Grampa."

Red Is the Color She Wore

Christmas Eve we bake bread, cookies, and make fudge. Posole with pig's feet and pork skins boils on the stove. Red chile is devoid of seed and stem and will later bubble in little erupting volcanoes. Tamales will be steamed. The Christmas tree lights and tinsel hang on the tree. For all that the world can tell, Christmas will be cheerful as usual.

Mom bought us dresses and new shoes. We bathe and prepare for midnight Mass. The phone rings. It is for Mom. She screams in disbelief. Dad takes the phone. A nurse asks, "Are you Mr. Tafoya?" Then, "You need to hurry. Fidel's blood clot has traveled to his lung."

My parents leave around 10:30 p.m. By the time they reach the hospital, Grampa has his wish. He is now in heaven with Grama to spend Christmas.

"You can't wear red to a funeral," Aunt Mary said to me. "Didn't you bring any other dress? Red is a happy color. Are you happy your grandpa died?"

Her stupid question is so small-minded. No. I wear no sackcloth nor do I cover myself in black from head to foot. I do not wail so loudly the neighbors can hear. My cry is monstrously silent.

I've lost my best friend, my hero, who rubbed his whiskers on my face while I screamed in joy and misery all at once. The funny guy who taught me checkers, Wajo, Cocinita, and so much more. He, who said he loved me, "Porque sí."